the art of non-sexual foreplay 2

a guide for women

Nolan Collins

Nolan Collins

contents

DISCLAIMER

The information contained within this book or my website is not a substitute for professional advice such as from a medical doctor, psychiatrist, therapist or counsellor. The information provided does not constitute legal or professional advice, nor is it intended to be.

Diagnosing psychological or medical conditions is for trained medical professionals (physicians and therapists).

Any decisions you make and the consequences thereof are your own. Under no circumstances can you hold Nolan Collins or RAMPIT Solutions Ltd liable for your actions.

I dedicate this book to all the women of the world who love their man and want to show him what love, connection and trust is all about. You know who you are. Keep doing what you're doing because we need you in our lives more than we often admit, or show. Thank you.

introduction

The Connection Men Secretly Crave

Let's address the unspoken truth about intimacy: None of us received a proper education in the art of emotional connection. When most people hear the word "foreplay," they immediately think of dimmed lights and brief fumbling before sex. But genuine foreplay—the kind that builds lasting intimacy and keeps desire alive—goes far beyond those limited moments.

Think about it. We dedicate years to learning calculus, memorising historical dates, and understanding economic theories, but somehow "How to Make Your Partner Feel Desired Without It Leading to Sex 101" never made it onto the curriculum. Instead, our education in intimacy often came from rom-coms where couples cycle between dramatic arguments and passionate bedroom scenes, or from awkward conversations with friends who were equally uninformed.

By adulthood, most of us are operating with:

- A belief that men only want physical intimacy that leads to sex
- A belief that you only have to show up for his little guy to show up
- A misunderstanding that men don't need or want emotional connection
- The relationship equivalent of a chef who only knows how to prepare one dish—and serves it repeatedly regardless of the occasion

Sensuality has become one of the great lost arts in modern relationships, particularly when directed toward men. Somewhere along the way, we've developed a cultural blindness to men's emotional and sensual needs. We've collectively decided that men should be satisfied with occasional physical affection and little else, creating a poverty of meaningful touch and appreciation that many men experience but few can articulate.

Men crave touch, appreciation, and sensual connection just as much as women do, but they've often been conditioned to suppress or deny these needs. And for the men who say they don't need these things, chances are they've simply adapted to their absence, having never experienced consistent, genuine appreciation and sensual connection.

Welcome to "The Art of Nonsexual Foreplay for Women," where we flip the script on what intimacy with men really means. It's the sum of a hundred small actions that make him feel seen, respected, and desired. It's the touch of your hand on his arm during conversation, the way you remember details about his day, and the lingering eye contact during quiet moments. These gestures aren't about manipulation or obligation; they're about connection.

This isn't just a book of tips and tricks; it's a guide to creating a relationship where your partner feels valued, seen, and understood in ways that deepen emotional and physical bonds without crossing into overtly sexual territory (though it may certainly lead there naturally). It's about mastering the subtle art of making someone feel desired in ways that resonate specifically with men.

Men don't want partners who only show up for the grand gestures or the obvious moments. They want someone who's present for the little things: the squeeze of a hand when confidence wavers, the appreciative glance across a room, the acknowledgment of efforts both large and small. They want someone who adds to their sense of self-worth rather than someone who expects them to derive all their validation internally.

Here's what's often misunderstood: intimacy doesn't start in the bedroom. It starts when he feels like he's the most important person in your world. It's built in those micro-moments when you notice him, show up for him, and communicate that you care. These gestures create the foundation for trust, safety, and connection—the true aphrodisiacs of any relationship.

The right kind of connection puts ego aside. You don't touch him, appreciate him, or acknowledge him to keep score or as a means to an end. Your gestures are clear, confident, and focused on him as an expression of genuine desire, respect, and attention. Men notice this. They feel it when your actions come from authentic appreciation rather than obligation or manipulation.

While the immediate goal of these actions isn't physical intimacy, it's the accumulation of these seemingly small habits that transforms your relationship over time. When physical intimacy does happen, it becomes infinitely more powerful because you've already established a language of connection. The ground between you is fertile with meaning, trust, and mutual understanding.

And the irony: the more you focus on making him feel safe, valued, and attractive, the more he'll naturally reciprocate. When you create a climate of appreciation, he'll respond in kind, and the touch, affection, and support you crave will flow more freely without you having to ask. It's not manipulation—it's connection. The better you make him feel about himself, the more positivity he'll reflect back to you.

Think of these gestures as compound interest for your relationship. Each small deposit might seem insignificant in the moment, but over time, they build a wealth of intimacy that pays dividends in every aspect of your connection. When moments of physical intimacy do arise, they're not isolated events but extensions of the connection you've been cultivating all along—richer, easier, and more profound because you've been practising intimacy in a hundred different ways.

Sensuality isn't about performance—it's about presence. It's not about what your friends say men want, or what social media portrays as ideal. It's about paying attention to his unique responses, learning his individual language of love. Maybe it's the way your hand on his shoulder relaxes him instantly. Maybe it's how your genuine laugh at his jokes lights him up from within. Or maybe it's just sitting beside him in comfortable silence with your leg gently touching his, or draped over him. The magic is in knowing that every small gesture counts when it's done with intention.

It's like trying to create a gourmet meal after only ever having cooked with a microwave. Sure, you know how to heat things up, but that doesn't qualify you to create a five-course dining experience. The result? Two people desperately wanting connection but having no idea how to create the delicious simmer of anticipation and appreciation that makes intimacy—both in and out of the bedroom—so much more satisfying.

And here's where it gets even better: once you've mastered these moments, you can take them deeper. Imagine the effect of these gestures when they become second nature. Imagine touching him gently as you pass by, making him feel like your attention naturally gravitates toward him. Or pausing during a hectic day to look at him with genuine appreciation, reinforcing that despite life's demands, he remains central in your thoughts. This isn't about grand performances—it's about making him your world through consistent, meaningful connection.

This book isn't just for women looking to enhance romantic relationships; it's for anyone who wants to understand how to nurture a connection with the men in their lives that feels alive, playful, and deeply meaningful. Whether you're in a new relationship or you've been married for years, the 75 gestures and accompanying insights in this book will help you turn ordinary moments into extraordinary connections.

So, take a breath. Slow down. Approach him not with calculation, but with the confidence of someone who knows that love, intimacy, and connection are built in the quiet moments. These gestures aren't about impressing him—they're about making him feel desired, adored, and truly seen. When you pay genuine attention to his needs and act with clarity and intention, you'll create a bond that deepens over time. Because in the end, the better you treat him, the better your relationship will feel for both of you.

It's never too late to learn that the most erogenous zone is actually the space between casual touch and sexual expectation—that delicious territory where intimacy thrives without demanding anything more. And it's never too early, or late, to start building the habits that make those moments of physical connection not just possible, but transcendent.

A Quick Word Before We Begin

Let's be crystal clear about something: this book assumes you're in a healthy, reciprocal relationship where both partners genuinely care about each other's wellbeing. These aren't instructions for becoming a 1950s housewife, subservient nodding machine, or ego-stroking service provider. If that's what someone's after, they've picked up the wrong book entirely (and possibly the wrong partner).

The whole point of these gestures is creating *and* enhancing genuine connection that benefits both of you. Think of them as relationship investments that pay dividends in the form of deeper understanding, mutual appreciation, and yes—a partner who's more likely to notice and respond to your needs as well.

The goal isn't creating a one-way street where you're constantly giving while he's constantly taking. It's about initiating positive cycles of attention and care where **both** people feel seen, valued, and motivated to contribute to each other's happiness.

Each gesture should leave you feeling good about the connection you've created—not drained, resentful, or wondering where your medal is and expecting a pat on the back!

When done authentically, these moments of attention create the foundation for the kind of relationship where thoughtfulness flows naturally in both directions, and both partners thrive in the warm glow of genuine appreciation.

⸻

If this book arrived as a gift from your partner, recognise it as appreciation for your existing love and attention, paired with interest in discovering fresh connection approaches. Consider it a compliment and opportunity to enhance what you already do well.

A note for men who discover this book at home:

If you realise certain meaningful gestures have originated from these pages, simply appreciate that your partner cares enough to actively nurture your relationship. If something particularly resonates that she hasn't tried, mention it conversationally (avoiding complaints like "you NEVER do..."). Then return the book discreetly and appreciate her intentional efforts to connect.

PS. If you want to know what you can do for her, and trust me, it's not the same as what she can do for you, then check out Book 1 of the Art of Nonsexual Foreplay - a guide for men - see the resources at the back of the book.

⊏⊐

Before we dive into the specifics, let's talk about how to make these actions work. Because while a thoughtful gesture can be powerful, how you deliver it is just as important as the gesture itself.

11 tips to make these gestures work better

LADIES, LET'S TALK ABOUT EXECUTION. JUST AS A CHEF NEEDS TO understand technique before creating a masterpiece, you need to grasp these fundamentals before your actions can truly resonate. Here's how to transform simple moments into powerful points of connection:

1. Master the Art of the Pause

Great connections aren't rushed. When you're about to touch his arm or meet his gaze with appreciation, pause for a beat. That moment of stillness heightens the significance of the gesture, giving him time to notice and feel its weight. A pause says, "I'm fully here with you." It also lets you gauge his response—whether he leans into the moment or needs a different approach.

Why it works: Anticipation amplifies the emotional impact of the action, making even small moments feel significant. That brief pause transforms an ordinary touch into a deliberate connection, showing him that this moment isn't casual—it's chosen.

2. Perfect the Power of Eye Contact

Eye contact isn't just looking at someone—it's seeing them. Hold his gaze for an extra second when you compliment him or during a quiet moment. This unspoken connection says everything words can't. But remember, no intense staring that might feel confrontational. This is intimacy, not an interrogation. If you're unsure, start small—catch his eye across the room and pair it with a warm smile that reaches your eyes.

Why it works: Eyes are a gateway to trust and vulnerability. Many women underestimate how rarely men receive the gift of being truly seen. Genuine eye contact says, "I'm interested in you, not just what you can do for me."

3. Touch with Intention

Not all touch is created equal. The difference between an incidental brush and a deliberate, lingering hand on his shoulder is profound. Think of touch like a spectrum: light brushes for playfulness, firm contact for reassurance, and everything in between for moments of connection. Even something as simple as tracing patterns on his palm can spark a feeling of closeness when done with care and presence.

Why it works: Thoughtful, intentional touch communicates care and attentiveness, signaling that you're fully present. Men can immediately sense the difference between absent-minded touching and deliberate connection, even if they don't articulate it.

4. Notice the Little Things

Did he get a haircut? Wear a new shirt? Mention something he's excited about? Noticing and bringing up these small details tells him, "I see you." It's not about flattery; it's about showing you're tuned in to his world. Something as simple as saying, "I like how that colour brings out your eyes," can make him feel appreciated in a way that resonates all day. The more specific your observation, the more powerful its impact.

Why it works: Feeling seen is one of the most powerful ways to build trust and connection. Men often feel invisible in their emotional and personal lives, with attention primarily on what they achieve or provide rather than who they are.

5. Let Silence Speak

Some of the most intimate moments don't need words. Resting your head against his shoulder, holding his hand, or simply sitting close says more than a thousand compliments ever could. Silence lets emotions breathe. It can also create a space for him to share what's on his mind without feeling rushed. Many women feel compelled to fill silence—resist this urge and discover the power of shared quiet.

Why it works: Stillness invites closeness and allows him to feel safe in your presence. It demonstrates security and confidence that many overlook in their rush to speak or act. For men who may struggle to articulate feelings, these quiet moments can be when they feel most connected.

6. Add Playfulness to the Mix

Romance isn't always serious. A spontaneous dance in the kitchen, a playful tease, or a shared laugh can bring lightness and warmth to your connection. Don't take yourself too seriously—fun is a cornerstone of intimacy. A quick moment of levity can ease tension and remind him that being with you is as enjoyable as it is meaningful.

Why it works: Playfulness creates both joy and safety. It tells him that not every interaction carries heavy expectations or potential criticism. This emotional safety is profoundly connecting for men, who often feel they must maintain composure or strength in other areas of life.

7. Be Receptive to His Gestures

When he makes an effort to connect, meet him more than halfway. Notice when he reaches out—whether through a small gift, a kind word, or physical affection—and respond with warmth and appreciation. This reciprocity creates a virtuous cycle where both of you feel increasingly safe to express affection.

Why it works: Men often test the waters with small gestures before risking greater vulnerability. When those initial efforts are warmly received, it encourages them to continue opening up. Conversely, if their gestures go unnoticed or are dismissed, they typically retreat emotionally.

8. Understand the Timing

Even the sweetest gesture can fall flat if poorly timed. If he's stressed or focused on a task, save certain approaches for when he can fully appreciate them. Thoughtfulness isn't just about what you do—it's about when you do it. For example, a lingering touch as he leaves for a stressful day might mean more than an elaborate gesture when he's distracted.

Why it works: Timing ensures your actions land with the impact they deserve. Men often compartmentalise, and recognising the right moment for connection shows respect for their process while still maintaining intimacy.

9. Be Consistent, Not Overwhelming

A single grand gesture is lovely, but consistent small actions are what truly build intimacy. Don't try to do all 75 gestures in one week—it's not a marathon. Pace yourself, and let these moments happen naturally. A pattern of thoughtfulness shows him you're present in his life for the long haul, not just performing to tick boxes.

Why it works: Steady care fosters trust and helps men feel secure in the relationship. Consistency signals that your attention isn't conditional on his performance or limited to when you want something from him.

10. Be Genuine

This one's simple: if you don't mean it, don't do it. Authenticity is the foundation of everything in this book. These gestures should reflect how you truly feel, not what you think you should do. Even a simple, heartfelt, "I'm so glad you're in my life," means more when it's genuine. Men have finely-tuned radars for insincerity—they'll sense it immediately if you're just going through the motions.

Why it works: Genuine actions resonate on a deeper level, making him feel truly valued. In a world full of performance and pretense, authenticity is the rarest and most precious gift you can offer.

11. Be Creative

The gestures and support sections are a guide for you to adapt and personalise. Think about all the things you appreciate about your partner. What attracted you to him? What makes him stand out? When you see the suggested phrases, don't use them verbatim if they feel awkward. Instead, think of something you would naturally say that will resonate more than a scripted phrase.

Why it works: Only you know your mind, and your partner. Getting creative opens up each gesture to more angles and ways to deliver them that work specifically for your unique relationship.

Remember, ladies: these aren't tricks or manipulations—they're skills. Like any worthwhile ability, they take practice and intention. The difference between someone who merely attempts these gestures and one who masters them is attention to these eleven fundamentals. Your relationship deserves that level of care.

Now, armed with these principles, let's explore the 75 gestures that will transform your relationship one thoughtful moment at a time.

understanding men's difficulty with receiving appreciation

Why He Might Deflect What He Deeply Desires

"Thanks, but it wasn't really a big deal." "You don't need to make a fuss about it." "I was just doing what needed to be done."

If you've ever complimented a man or expressed gratitude for his efforts only to have him downplay or dismiss your appreciation, you've witnessed one of the most common and puzzling disconnects in male-female dynamics. This tendency to deflect genuine appreciation isn't just modest humility—it's the result of complex cultural conditioning and emotional patterns that most men aren't even conscious of.

Understanding this contradiction—that men simultaneously crave appreciation while often appearing uncomfortable receiving it—is crucial to creating the kind of connection that resonates deeply. Let's explore why this happens and how to navigate it effectively.

The Hidden Hunger for Recognition

Men are typically raised with messages that emphasise stoicism, self-sufficiency, and emotional restraint. From early childhood, many boys are taught explicitly or implicitly that:

• Needing acknowledgment is a sign of weakness or insecurity

• Their value lies primarily in what they achieve or provide

• Emotional needs should be minimised or suppressed

• Accepting praise can appear vain or self-important

• Vulnerability risks rejection or judgment

These messages create a profound paradox. On one hand, men deeply desire to be seen, appreciated, and valued for who they are and what they contribute. On the other hand, they've been conditioned to appear unmoved by this need, sometimes even to themselves.

Research consistently shows that feeling appreciated ranks among the top emotional needs for men in relationships, yet they're often the least equipped to receive it gracefully. This isn't a character flaw—it's a predictable outcome of how most boys are socialised.

Why He Deflects Your Appreciation

When you offer genuine appreciation and he deflects it, several factors may be at play:

1. Protection from Disappointment

If he allows himself to fully receive and value your appreciation, he also becomes vulnerable to its absence or withdrawal. Minimising its importance is a subconscious defence mechanism against potential future hurt.

2. Discomfort with Attention

Many men are taught that drawing attention to themselves is inappropriate or self-centred. Your focus on him, even when positive, can trigger this discomfort.

3. Unworthiness Beliefs

Some men carry deep-seated beliefs that they don't deserve praise or affection unless they've done something extraordinary. Everyday appreciation can conflict with these beliefs, creating confusing and conflicting beliefs and behaviour.

4. Fear of Increased Expectations

Accepting praise for an action or quality can create anxiety that he'll now be expected to maintain or exceed that standard consistently.

5. Limited Emotional Vocabulary

Many men simply haven't developed the emotional language and skills to process and express gratitude for appreciation. Their awkwardness is often misinterpreted as disinterest.

6. Confusion About Intentions

Unfortunately, some men have experienced appreciation being used manipulatively in past relationships. This can create suspicion about sincere expressions of gratitude or admiration.

How to Navigate His Resistance

Despite these barriers, your appreciation is not only valued but essential. The key is understanding how to offer it in ways he can receive:

Be Specific and Factual

General compliments like "You're amazing" are easier to dismiss than specific observations like "The way you handled that difficult conversation with the neighbour showed real diplomacy." Specificity makes appreciation harder to deflect and more meaningful to receive.

Connect to Impact

Explain how his actions or qualities affect you personally: "When you remembered that small detail about my work project, it made me feel so supported and understood." This shifts the focus from his worthiness (which he may question) to your experience (which he can't dispute).

Offer Without Expectation

Appreciation given with an apparent agenda will likely be met with wariness. Ensure your expressions of gratitude and admiration are freely given, with no strings attached.

Be Consistent but Unpredictable

Regular appreciation builds trust in its sincerity, while unpredictability prevents it from feeling routine or obligatory. Surprise him with recognition at unexpected moments.

Respect His Response

If he deflects or seems uncomfortable, don't insist he accept your appreciation in the way you think he should. Instead, deliver your message clearly but allow him to process it in his own way.

Use Physical Touch as Reinforcement

For many men, physical connection can bypass verbal defences. A squeeze of the hand or a touch on the arm while expressing appreciation can help the message penetrate more deeply.

The Gradual Transformation

With consistent, thoughtful appreciation, most men gradually develop greater capacity to receive it. You may notice subtle shifts over time:

- Less immediate deflection or denial

- More direct eye contact when you express gratitude

- Increased reciprocal expressions of appreciation

- Greater willingness to share his own needs and desires

- A general softening in his emotional responses

These changes don't typically happen overnight. They're the result of creating a reliable climate of appreciation where he learns, sometimes for the first time, that his deeper emotional needs are safe to acknowledge and express.

When Deeper Barriers Exist

If your partner shows extreme discomfort with appreciation that doesn't ease over time, or if he consistently responds with suspicion or anger, deeper issues may be at play. Childhood emotional neglect, previous relationship trauma, or significant attachment wounds can create more substantial barriers to receiving positive feedback. In these cases, professional support may be beneficial for both of you.

Remember Your Own Worth

While understanding his difficulty receiving appreciation is important, be mindful not to fall into patterns where your genuine expressions are consistently invalidated. Your desire to acknowledge and appreciate him is valuable and worthy of respect, even as he learns to receive it more openly.

A healthy dynamic involves mutual growth—him developing greater capacity to receive appreciation, and you learning the particular ways he can best accept it. This dance of giving and receiving creates the foundation for the deeper connection that the gestures in this book are designed to nurture.

As we move forward into the specific gestures, carry this understanding with you. When your appreciation appears to bounce off him or get deflected, know that it's still having an impact—sometimes in ways neither of you can immediately see. The seeds you plant through consistent, sincere recognition often grow quietly before their effects become visible.

With this awareness as our foundation, let's explore the 75 gestures that will help you create the climate of appreciation and connection that allows both of you to thrive.

one

placing your hand on the back of his neck during conversation

Why It Helps

THERE ARE FEW SPOTS ON THE MALE BODY THAT COMBINE vulnerability and strength quite like the back of the neck. When you gently rest your hand there during conversation, you're connecting with both the protector and the human being who occasionally needs protection himself. This gesture creates an instant sense of intimacy and grounding without a single word spoken.

The back of the neck is rarely touched in casual interaction, making your connection there feel exclusive and deliberate. For many men, this area carries tension from stress and responsibility. Your touch provides both acknowledgment of that burden and momentary relief from it. It's as if you're saying, "I see the weight you carry, and I'm here with you."

There's also something quietly possessive about this gesture that most men respond to positively. Not possessive in a controlling way, but in a way that says, "You are mine to care for; you matter specifically to me."

Phrase to Say

"I love talking with you like this." OR "I just want to feel connected while we talk."

Tips to Make It Work

- **Eye Contact:** Maintain gentle eye contact while your hand rests on his neck. This dual connection —physical touch with visual attention—creates a powerful circuit of intimacy.
- **Pressure:** Keep your touch light but definite. Too feathery may tickle or feel hesitant; too firm might seem controlling. Aim for a warmth and weight that feels grounding.
- **Duration:** This isn't a pat or quick squeeze, but a lingering connection. Allow your hand to rest there for at least several seconds, or throughout a meaningful part of your conversation.

When to Use

This gesture works beautifully during important conversations where you want to emphasise connection alongside content. Also when he's sharing something meaningful, when you're discussing relationship matters, or during moments of reconciliation after discord.

It can also serve as a powerful pattern interrupt if you notice him beginning to intellectualise or disconnect from a conversation that would benefit from emotional presence. The physical connection often helps bring him back to the present moment.

squeezing his forearm gently in conversation

Why It Helps

THE FOREARM REPRESENTS A PERFECT MIDDLE GROUND IN PHYSICAL connection—more intimate than touching a shoulder, less charged than touching a thigh. When you gently squeeze his forearm during conversation, you're creating a physical punctuation mark that says, "This moment matters. You matter. I'm fully here with you."

This gesture works on multiple levels. Physically, the forearm contains fewer nerve endings than areas like hands or face, making it a comfortable place for men who might be touch-sensitive. Psychologically, it creates connection without vulnerability, allowing him to maintain his composure while still feeling your presence. Emotionally, it serves as a nonverbal reminder of your attention and care.

Phrase to Say

This gesture often works best without words, letting the touch speak for itself. If anything, perhaps: "I'm really enjoying this conversation." OR simply meeting his eyes warmly as you squeeze.

Tips to Make It Work

- **Timing:** Coordinate the squeeze with meaningful moments in conversation—when he shares something important, when you want to emphasise a point, or when you're expressing agreement or support.
- **Pressure:** Apply gentle but definite pressure that he can feel through a shirt sleeve. Too light might feel uncertain; too firm could be distracting.
- **Duration:** Keep the squeeze brief but deliberate—approximately two to three seconds—long enough to register as intentional but not so long that it becomes the focus rather than the complement to your conversation.

When to Use

This gesture creates beautiful connection during everyday conversations, when sharing meals, while walking side by side, or during social gatherings when you want to create a private moment of connection within a public setting. It's particularly effective when you notice him expressing something meaningful but downplaying its importance— the squeeze communicates, "I caught that, and it matters."

sending an unprompted text telling him what you admire about him

Why It Helps

AN UNPROMPTED MESSAGE OF ADMIRATION LANDS LIKE AN unexpected gift. Unlike texts about logistics, schedules, or needs, a message that specifically expresses what you admire about him creates a moment of pure appreciation without the expectation of anything in return. This digital gesture says, "You crossed my mind not because I need something, but because I value who you are."

The unprompted nature is what makes this particularly powerful. Written appreciation also gives him something he can return to and reread. Many men privately revisit such messages during challenging moments or times of self-doubt, drawing strength from your expressed admiration even when you're not physically present.

Phrase to Say

"I was just thinking about how you always find solutions where others see only problems. " OR "The way you spoke up for that new person at work yesterday showed such character. I'm constantly impressed by your integrity."

Tips to Make It Work

- **Specificity:** Focus on a particular quality, action, or character trait rather than general praise. "I admire your patience with your mother" carries more impact than "You're such a good son."
- **Sincerity:** Only express admiration you genuinely feel. Inauthentic praise will likely feel hollow.
- **Timing:** Send it during his workday or the afternoon when you're apart, creating a bridge of connection across physical separation.

When to Use

This gesture is perfect for ordinary days—not just special occasions. It's particularly powerful during periods when he's facing challenges, when work or other commitments have created some distance between you, or simply when you notice something admirable about him that you haven't expressed recently.

The beauty of this gesture is that it requires no special circumstance—any day is the right day to express genuine admiration. That said, be mindful not to overuse it. Like any meaningful gesture, its impact comes partly from its thoughtful deployment rather than constant repetition.

four
noticing and complimenting a subtle change in his appearance

Why It Helps

MEN OFTEN MAKE EFFORTS WITH THEIR APPEARANCE THAT GO completely unacknowledged. When you notice and comment on a subtle change—a new haircut, a different style of shirt, trimmed facial hair, even particularly clean shoes—you're demonstrating an attentiveness that most men rarely experience. This gesture says, "I see the details of you, not just the obvious parts."

What makes this especially meaningful is how it counters a common male experience. Many men feel simultaneously invisible and assessed in daily life—noticed for their utility or performance but not for their personal choices or aesthetic efforts. Your specific observation breaks through this pattern, creating a moment of being truly seen.

There's also intimacy in noticing what others miss. While anyone might comment on dramatic changes, observing subtle shifts requires genuine attention and familiarity. It confirms that you're paying attention at a level that casual observers don't reach.

Phrase to Say

"That new haircut really suits you—I like how it frames your face." OR "Is that shirt new? The colour brings out your eyes in a way I've never noticed before."

Tips to Make It Work

- **Specificity:** Note exactly what has changed and why it works well rather than just acknowledging that something's different.
- **Timing:** Offer the compliment relatively soon after noticing the change, when it's still fresh enough to be relevant but not so immediately that it seems reflexive.
- **Sincerity:** Only comment positively if you genuinely appreciate the change. Inauthentic compliments are easily detected and can undermine trust.

When to Use

This gesture works perfectly after he visits the barber, when he wears something new or different, when he makes an effort for an occasion, or even when he's particularly well-groomed on an ordinary day. The key is consistent attention to these details, not just noticing dramatic changes.

actively listening to his story without interrupting

Why It Helps

Few gifts are as valuable as undivided attention, yet in our distraction-filled world, it's become increasingly rare. When you actively listen to him share a story or experience without interrupting, checking your phone, or mentally preparing your response, you're creating a space of respect that many men rarely encounter. This attentive presence says, "What you have to say matters to me. You have my full attention."

This addresses a common experience: being listened to for content but not for connection. Men are often heard for information or solutions they provide but less often listened to simply because their experience and perspective matter. Your complete attention fills this emotional gap.

Many conversations become subtle competitions for airtime, with interruptions signaling that the listener's thoughts take priority over the speaker's experience.

Phrase to Say

After he finishes: "Thank you for sharing that with me." OR "I love hearing about your experiences/thoughts/day."

Tips to Make It Work

- **Body Language:** Turn toward him physically, maintain comfortable eye contact, and offer non-verbal cues (nodding, responsive expressions) that show engagement without taking over.
- **Patience:** Allow for his pauses and thinking time without jumping in. Some men process verbally and need space to formulate thoughts mid-story.
- **Questions:** Ask clarifying or deepening questions that follow his narrative thread rather than redirecting to your interests or experiences.

When to Use

This gesture creates connection during everyday conversations about work challenges, personal projects, childhood memories, or current interests. It's particularly valuable when he's processing something difficult, sharing an accomplishment, or expressing enthusiasm about a subject important to him—moments when being truly heard contributes significantly to feeling valued and understood. It requires no special circumstance—any conversation becomes an opportunity for meaningful connection through attentive listening.

six

touching the small of his back as you pass by

Why It Helps

THIS BRIEF POINT OF CONTACT AS YOU MOVE THROUGH SHARED space creates a moment of connection without demanding response. The small of the back is an intimate yet non-intrusive area that signals affection while respecting his space. This touch says, "I'm aware of you even in transition; you remain in my consciousness even during mundane moments."

What elevates this gesture beyond casual contact is its deliberate nature. Unlike accidental brushes, this intentional touch transforms an ordinary passing into an opportunity for connection, turning functional movement into an expression of ongoing awareness and appreciation.

Phrase to Say

This gesture works beautifully without words, letting the touch speak for itself. If anything, perhaps a soft "Excuse me" or gentle "Mmm" of appreciation.

Tips to Make It Work

- **Pressure:** Keep your touch light but definite—firm enough to register through clothing but gentle enough to feel like affection rather than guidance.
- **Duration:** Allow your hand to linger just slightly longer than necessary for simply passing by, but briefly enough to respect his ongoing activity.
- **Eye Contact:** A quick glance or small smile as you touch him enhances the connection without interrupting his focus.

When to Use

This gesture creates lovely connection during domestic activities—while cooking together, passing in hallways, or navigating shared morning routines. It's particularly effective during busy periods when extended interaction isn't possible, creating brief but meaningful points of contact amid separate activities.

greeting him with genuine enthusiasm when he returns home

Why It Helps

THE TRANSITION FROM OUTSIDE WORLD TO HOME IS SIGNIFICANT—a daily threshold between public performance and private self. When you greet him with genuine enthusiasm, you're acknowledging this transition and welcoming not just his physical presence but his complete self. This reception says, "Your arrival matters to me; home is different—better—when you're in it."

This gesture addresses the common male experience of feeling functionally invisible unless performing or providing. Your enthusiastic acknowledgment counters this pattern, affirming that his simple presence has inherent value beyond what he does or brings.

Phrase to Say

"There you are! I'm so glad you're home." OR "Hey you! I missed you today," accompanied by genuine warmth in your expression.

Tips to Make It Work

- **Authenticity:** Ensure your enthusiasm comes from genuine pleasure rather than performance. Brief but real connection surpasses elaborate but forced greeting.
- **Physical Presence:** If possible, pause what you're doing to create a proper greeting—even 30 seconds of full attention creates powerful recognition.
- **Adaptation:** Match your greeting to his energy when appropriate. If he's clearly depleted, your enthusiasm might be gentler but still warmly welcoming.

When to Use

This gesture applies whenever either of you returns home after separation—whether from work, travel, or just errands. It's particularly meaningful after challenging days when the contrast between outside stress and home welcome provides significant emotional regulation and reconnection.

preparing his favourite comfort food as a surprise

Why It Helps

FOOD PREPARED SPECIFICALLY WITH SOMEONE'S PREFERENCES IN mind carries emotional significance far beyond nutrition. When you make his favourite comfort food without being asked, you're communicating thorough knowledge of what brings him pleasure and willingness to transform that knowledge into tangible care. This thoughtful gesture says, "I pay attention to what comforts you, and I'll create that experience simply for your enjoyment."

The surprise element amplifies the impact, showing that your care isn't merely responsive to requests but proactively attuned to his needs and preferences. It demonstrates both attentiveness to what he enjoys and initiative in creating moments of unexpected pleasure.

Phrase to Say

"I made your favourite pasta—thought you might enjoy it

tonight." OR "I remembered how much you love this dish and wanted to surprise you."

Tips to Make It Work

- **Memory:** Prepare something he has specifically mentioned enjoying in the past or that you've observed bringing him particular satisfaction.
- **Timing:** Choose a moment when he can actually enjoy it without rush or distraction rather than when he's heading out or preoccupied.
- **Presentation:** Serve it with simple acknowledgment rather than fanfare that might create pressure to perform appropriate levels of gratitude.

When to Use

This gesture works wonderfully after particularly demanding days, during periods of stress, when celebrating accomplishments, or simply as an unexpected pleasure on an ordinary evening. The ordinariness of the occasion often makes it more special than saving such gestures only for traditional gift-giving moments.

initiating a lingering hug when he least expects it

Why It Helps

IN THE RHYTHM OF DAILY LIFE, PHYSICAL AFFECTION OFTEN becomes routinised or brief—quick hugs, perfunctory kisses, habitual touches. When you initiate a lingering hug at an unexpected moment, you break this pattern, creating a sudden island of connection in the stream of ordinary interaction. This embrace says, "This moment—you—deserve more than passing acknowledgment; you deserve full presence."

What distinguishes this from routine hugs is both duration and quality. A lingering hug, held long enough for bodies to relax and breathing to synchronise, triggers physiological calm through oxytocin release while creating psychological reassurance through sustained connection.

Phrase to Say

"I just needed to hold you for a minute." OR Simply allow

the hug to speak for itself, perhaps with a contented sigh or hum of appreciation.

Tips to Make It Work

- **Wholeness:** Engage your full body in the embrace rather than partial contact—this complete connection carries greater impact.
- **Presence:** Bring your full attention to the hug, noticing the sensations of contact, warmth, and gradually relaxing tension.
- **Patience:** Allow the hug to find its natural conclusion rather than abruptly cutting it short or artificially extending it.

When to Use

This gesture creates beautiful connection during ordinary moments when affection isn't necessarily expected—while he's working on a project, after he completes a household task, or during a casual conversation. The unexpectedness during mundane activities is what creates its impact, transforming ordinary time into meaningful connection.

ten
writing him a note expressing specific appreciation

Why It Helps

IN A WORLD DOMINATED BY DIGITAL COMMUNICATION, A handwritten note carries distinct significance. When you take time to write specific appreciation by hand, you're transforming momentary acknowledgment into something tangible and lasting. This deliberate gesture says, "My appreciation deserves more than passing mention; it deserves to be captured and preserved."

Handwritten notes also provide men something they rarely receive—appreciation they can revisit privately. Many men keep such notes for years, sometimes decades, returning to them during moments of doubt or difficulty as tangible evidence of their value and impact.

Other times they may revisit to remind themselves how special you are for doing something so unique and thoughtful.

Phrase to Say

"Your patience during that challenging family dinner made all the difference. I noticed and deeply appreciated how you stayed calm and supportive through the chaos." OR "The way you remember details about my friends shows such thoughtfulness. It means more to me than you might realise."

Tips to Make It Work

- **Specificity:** Focus on a particular quality, action, or pattern you genuinely appreciate rather than generic praise.
- **Placement:** Leave your note where he'll find it privately—in his wallet, laptop bag, or on his pillow—creating a moment of discovery without audience or expectation.
- **Simplicity:** Keep it concise and direct rather than elaborate—the fact that you've written by hand already communicates special effort.

When to Use

This gesture creates meaningful connection after you've observed something particularly admirable, during challenging periods when verbal affirmation might get lost in stress, before separations like business trips, or simply as an unexpected affirmation on an ordinary day. The surprise of finding tangible appreciation when he least expects it amplifies its emotional impact.

"The best thing to hold
onto in life is each
other." - Audrey
Hepburn

Nolan Collins

The first ten gestures in this collection share a fundamental truth: connection is built through the deliberate choice to reach for each other, again and again. Whether it's the gentle pressure of your hand on the back of his neck during conversation, the enthusiastic greeting when he comes home, or the lingering hug that says "I'm fully here with you"—each gesture represents an active decision to hold onto what matters most.

These aren't grand romantic gestures but everyday choices to prioritise connection over convenience, presence over productivity. When you squeeze his forearm during conversation or write him a note expressing specific appreciation, you're essentially reaching across the ordinary moments of life to remind him: "You are worth holding onto."

eleven
looking at him with desire across a room

Why It Helps

A DELIBERATELY APPRECIATIVE GAZE FROM ACROSS A ROOM CREATES a private moment of connection amid public space. When you look at him with unmistakable desire—not just casual acknowledgment—you're establishing an intimate circuit that exists regardless of physical distance or social context. This visual connection says, "Even surrounded by others, I see you specifically and find you deeply attractive."

This gesture is particularly powerful because it cuts through men's common experience of feeling generically observed rather than particularly desired. Your gaze, laden with genuine appreciation, counters this pattern, confirming that he is not just noticed but actively wanted.

Phrase to Say

This gesture requires no words—the look itself communicates everything necessary. If your eyes meet and hold, perhaps a slight smile or subtle lip bite can enhance the message without overplaying it.

Tips to Make It Work

- **Duration:** Allow your gaze to linger just long enough to register as deliberate, but not so long it becomes uncomfortable or obvious to others.
- **Authenticity:** Ensure your look comes from genuine appreciation rather than performance— men can typically distinguish between real desire and theatrical display.
- **Context:** Across a dinner table, at a social gathering, or even in your own home while engaged in separate activities—the key is the deliberate choice to connect visually amid other possibilities.

When to Use

This gesture creates beautiful connection during social gatherings, family events, or even ordinary evenings at home. It's particularly effective when he might be feeling overlooked, when he's done something quietly impressive without fanfare, or simply when you're struck by genuine appreciation for him amid the flow of daily life.

twelve
resting your head on his shoulder without saying a word

WHY IT HELPS

Physical interdependence communicates trust in ways words often can't. When you rest your head on his shoulder, you're creating a moment where your literal balance relies on his support. This gesture of physical trust says, "I feel safe with you; I choose to lean on your strength."

What makes this especially meaningful for many men is how it acknowledges their capacity to provide support without demanding action or solution. It's pure acceptance of their presence as valuable—allowing them to simply be rather than do.

Phrase to Say

This gesture works best without words, letting the physical connection speak for itself. If anything, perhaps a contented sigh or soft "Mmm" of appreciation.

Tips to Make It Work

Weight: Allow genuine relaxation—actually resting your weight rather than barely touching—this creates authentic connection rather than symbolic contact.

Timing: Choose moments when he's available for connection, not actively engaged in tasks requiring movement or concentration.

Duration: Let this contact last long enough to feel like genuine seeking of closeness rather than momentary acknowledgment.

When to Use

This gesture creates lovely connection during quiet moments together—while watching television, sitting on a park bench, or during a lull in conversation. It's particularly effective during times of emotional fatigue when words might feel inadequate or effortful for either of you.

thirteen

laughing genuinely at his humour

WHY IT HELPS

Humour represents one of the more vulnerable forms of self-expression, especially for men who often use it to connect indirectly. When you laugh genuinely at his jokes or witty observations, you're validating not just the specific attempt at humour but his unique perspective and way of engaging with the world. This authentic response says, "I get you—your particular way of seeing things resonates with me."

What distinguishes this from polite response is its authenticity. A genuine laugh—eyes crinkling, spontaneous sound, real amusement—communicates connection on a level beyond courtesy. It confirms shared wavelength, creating a private circuit of mutual understanding.

Phrase to Say

The laugh itself is what matters here—natural, unforced, and proportionate to the level of humour. If adding words, perhaps: "You always make me laugh" or "I love how you see things."

Tips to Make It Work

Authenticity: Only laugh when genuinely amused—insincere laughter is quickly detected and undermines trust rather than building it.

Engagement: When possible, build on his humour occasionally—adding to the joke, referencing it later, or creating running gags from particularly memorable ones.

Appreciation: Let your enjoyment show physically—not just polite chuckles but full engagement with his comedic offerings.

When to Use

This gesture is perfect anytime he makes a joke, obviously, but carries particular weight when he tries something new, takes a risk with edgier humour, or seems slightly self-conscious about his attempt. Your warm reception in these vulnerable moments builds significant trust.

fourteen
touching his face gently with appreciation

WHY IT HELPS

The face represents one of our most vulnerable and expressive areas—literally the part of ourselves we present to the world. When you touch his face with gentle appreciation, you're connecting with his most exposed self. This intimate gesture says, "I cherish not just what you do, but who you fundamentally are."

What makes this particularly meaningful is its focus on his personhood rather than function or role. Unlike acknowledgment of achievements or abilities, this touch honours his essential being—the man himself rather than his actions or contributions.

Phrase to Say

"Sometimes I just need to touch you." OR "You have the most expressive face."

Tips to Make It Work

Gentleness: Use the lightest possible touch—a finger tracing his jawline, a palm resting briefly against his cheek, or brushing back a stray hair from his forehead.

Eye Contact: Maintain gentle eye connection during this gesture, creating dual pathways of intimacy through touch and gaze.

Presence: Bring full attention to this moment rather than touching absentmindedly while focused elsewhere.

When to Use

This gesture creates profound connection during quiet moments together—after meaningful conversations, during peaceful silences, or transitional times like morning awakening or evening winding down. It's particularly powerful when offered without expectation or demand— purely as an expression of appreciation for his presence in your life.

fifteen

using his shoulder as a pillow during a film

WHY IT HELPS

Creating physical interdependence during shared activities establishes a subtle but powerful message of trust and preference. When you use his shoulder as a pillow while watching a film, you're communicating both comfort with closeness and specific desire for his proximity. This positioning says, "Of all possible positions, I choose one that connects us. Your body is my preferred resting place."

The extended duration of this contact distinguishes it from momentary touches. Settling in against him for the length of a film creates sustained connection, allowing both of you to experience extended physical proximity without the expectation of escalation or response.

Phrase to Say

"You make the perfect pillow." OR "Is it okay if I get comfortable against you?" though often the gesture needs no verbal accompaniment.

Tips to Make It Work

Comfort: Find a position that's genuinely sustainable rather than one that looks intimate but creates physical strain over time.

Receptivity: Be attentive to his response—adjusting if you sense discomfort or leaning more fully into the connection if he welcomes it.

Presence: While focusing primarily on the film, occasional moments of acknowledged connection—a squeeze of the hand, a contented sigh—enhance the intimacy.

When to Use

This gesture works beautifully during home film nights, long car journeys where you're the passenger, or any shared sedentary activity. It's particularly effective during otherwise ordinary evenings, transforming routine activities into opportunities for physical closeness and comfort.

sixteen

telling him specifically how he makes you feel safe

WHY IT HELPS

The ability to provide safety—emotional, physical, or practical—resonates deeply with most men's sense of purpose. When you specifically articulate how he creates safety for you, you're acknowledging a core aspect of his identity and contribution. This verbal recognition says, "Your strength has real impact; your presence makes a tangible difference in my experience."

Unlike general statements like "You make me feel good," specific acknowledgment of safety touches something fundamental. It validates not just what he does but an essential quality of his presence and its meaningful effect on your wellbeing.

Phrase to Say

"When you handled that difficult conversation with the landlord, I felt so protected. You create space where I don't have to carry everything alone." OR "The way you stay calm when I'm anxious helps me feel grounded and safe."

Tips to Make It Work

Specificity: Identify exactly how he creates safety—through physical presence, emotional steadiness, practical problem-solving, or consistent reliability.

Authenticity: Only express this for genuine experiences of safety; manufactured acknowledgment will feel hollow to both of you.

Vulnerability: Allow yourself to be authentic about valuing this aspect of his nature, even if part of you feels it shouldn't matter in modern relationships.

When to Use

This gesture creates profound connection after situations where his protective qualities have been evident, during quiet moments of appreciation, or when you genuinely reflect on the value of his presence in your life. It's particularly meaningful when offered spontaneously rather than as response to his actions or requests for validation.

seventeen

creating a moment of peace when he's stressed

WHY IT HELPS

Men often shoulder stress with minimal outward indication, maintaining composure even while experiencing significant internal pressure. When you proactively create a pocket of peace during stressful periods, you're acknowledging the weight he carries without requiring him to articulate or justify it. This thoughtful gesture says, "I notice your stress even when you don't name it, and your wellbeing matters to me."

What makes this especially meaningful is how it addresses a common male experience: the expectation to manage difficulty without support unless explicitly requested. Your initiative in creating peace without being asked counters this isolation, offering connection precisely when it's most needed but often least requested.

Phrase to Say

"Let's take fifteen minutes to just breathe before dealing

with the rest of this." OR "I've handled those calls you were worried about. Come sit with me for a bit."

Tips to Make It Work

Observation: Watch for subtle signs of stress—tightened jaw, shortened breath, increased intensity—rather than waiting for obvious signals.

Environment: Create actual spaciousness through reduced stimulation—lowered voices, minimal requirements, physical comfort—rather than just encouraging relaxation verbally.

Presence: Offer calm companionship without demanding conversation or processing, allowing him to recalibrate without social performance.

When to Use

This gesture creates meaningful support during work pressure, after difficult interactions, when facing challenging decisions, or amid ongoing life stressors. It's particularly valuable when applied consistently during both major and minor stress periods, creating reliable respite rather than occasional rescue.

eighteen
brushing your fingers through his hair while he relaxes

Why It Helps

Gentle scalp stimulation creates a unique combination of pleasure, relaxation, and intimate care. When you brush your fingers through his hair while he's relaxed, you're creating sensory pleasure that requires nothing from him in return. This nurturing touch says, "You deserve care simply for being, not for doing or providing."

What distinguishes this from more casual touch is its giving nature. Unlike touches that request or initiate interaction, this gesture is purely about offering comfort and connection without expectation. It allows him to simply receive—an experience many men have too rarely.

Phrase to Say

This gesture often needs no words, letting the sensation speak for itself. If anything, perhaps: "I love the feel of your hair." OR "Is this relaxing for you?" spoken softly.

Tips to Make It Work

Technique: Use gentle pressure directly against the scalp in small, circular motions rather than just skimming the surface of the hair.

Attention: Watch for signals of what pressure and rhythm he finds most pleasant, as preferences vary significantly.

Consistency: Once you begin, maintain the touch for at least several minutes rather than brief or interrupted contact.

When to Use

This gesture creates beautiful connection during quiet evenings together, while watching television, during conversation, or as part of helping him unwind before sleep. It's particularly effective when he seems mentally preoccupied or physically tense, offering nonverbal permission to release the day's accumulated stress.

nineteen
bringing him his favourite drink without being asked

WHY IT HELPS

Anticipating needs before they're expressed demonstrates both attentiveness and proactive care. When you bring him his favourite drink without prompting, you're showing that you've internalised his preferences and take pleasure in meeting them. This thoughtful gesture says, "I pay attention to what brings you pleasure, and I care enough to create that experience unprompted."

Unlike responding to requests, which can sometimes feel transactional, anticipating desires communicates a deeper level of consideration. It shows you're thinking about his comfort even when he hasn't articulated a need, creating a moment of being genuinely seen and valued.

Phrase to Say

"Thought you might enjoy this." OR Simply offer the drink with a warm smile, letting the gesture speak for itself.

Tips to Make It Work

Timing: Choose moments when a drink would be genuinely welcome—after he's been working on a project, just as he sits down to relax, or when you notice subtle signs of thirst.

Memory: Prepare it exactly as he prefers—temperature, strength, accompanying ice or garnish—showing that you've noted these details.

Casualness: Offer it naturally rather than with fanfare that might create pressure to perform appropriate levels of gratitude.

When to Use

This gesture creates lovely connection during ordinary evenings at home, while he's engaged in projects or activities, after he returns from outside exertion, or during relaxed social occasions. Its power lies in unpredictability —not a routine service but a spontaneous expression of care that shows ongoing attentiveness.

twenty
sharing a private joke that connects just the two of you

WHY IT HELPS

Shared humour that references experiences or observations only the two of you understand creates a powerful boundary of intimacy. When you bring up or create private jokes, you're affirming the unique world that exists between you, accessible to no one else. This exclusive connection says, "We share a perspective and history that's ours alone—I value that private universe we've built."

The privacy of the reference is what makes this especially meaningful. Unlike general humour, these moments tap into shared knowledge, cementing the bond of your specific connection. They remind both of you that regardless of who else is present, you share something unique and valuable.

Phrase to Say

This varies entirely based on your specific shared references, but might be as simple as a catchphrase from a memorable experience, a raised eyebrow recalling a previous conversation, or a word that holds special meaning in your private vocabulary.

Tips to Make It Work

Subtlety: Often the most powerful shared moments are conveyed through the smallest signals—a specific word, a particular look, a barely perceptible gesture.

History: Draw from genuinely shared experiences rather than manufacturing inside jokes—authentic connection comes from real shared history.

Evolution: Allow these references to evolve and multiply over time, creating an increasingly rich private language between you.

When to Use

This gesture creates beautiful connection during social gatherings where a private moment feels particularly special, during otherwise ordinary conversations where a shared reference adds depth, or when either of you could use reminder of your unique bond. It's particularly valuable during challenging periods, reinforcing connection through humour when other forms of intimacy might feel strained.

Being deeply loved by
someone gives you
strength, while loving
someone deeply gives you
courage. - Lao Tzu

Nolan Collins

These last ten gestures demonstrate the courage required to love openly—the bravery to look at him with desire across a room, to rest your head on his shoulder without words, to touch his face with genuine appreciation. When you laugh authentically at his humour or use his shoulder as a pillow during a film, you're showing him what it means to be deeply loved. In return, his growing confidence in your appreciation gives him the strength to be more vulnerable, more present, more himself. This is the beautiful reciprocity of intentional love—your courage to express appreciation creates his strength to receive it.

twenty-one
asking him to teach you something he's passionate about

Why It Helps

Few requests are as affirming as a genuine invitation to share expertise or passion. When you ask him to teach you something he cares about, you're validating both his knowledge and his enthusiasm as worthy of attention. This request says, "I value what you know and love; I want to understand this part of your world."

What makes this particularly meaningful is its acknowledgment of his mastery. Many men develop deep knowledge in specific areas without regular opportunities to share that expertise in ways that feel appreciated rather than tedious or showing off. Your genuine interest creates space for him to share competence without apology.

Phrase to Say

"Would you show me how you manage to get such beautiful photos with your camera? I'd love to understand what you're looking for when you shoot." OR "I've always been curious about how you create those amazing sauces when you cook—would you teach me your approach sometime?"

Tips to Make It Work

Authenticity: Only ask about subjects where you have genuine curiosity—manufactured interest is quickly detected and feels patronising.

Engagement: Show active attention through questions and observations rather than passive presence.

Patience: Allow him to share at his own pace and depth without rushing or simplifying the experience.

When to Use

This gesture creates beautiful connection when you notice him engaged in activities he enjoys, when he mentions interests in passing, or when you observe skills he demonstrates without fanfare. It's particularly effective for subjects he rarely gets to discuss in depth with others, creating space for passion that might otherwise remain private.

twenty-two
playing with his fingers while talking

WHY IT HELPS

Casual, playful touch during conversation creates a physical connection that enhances emotional intimacy without demanding response. When you play with his fingers while talking—tracing patterns, gently manipulating joints, or simply holding while your thumb moves—you're establishing tactile connection alongside verbal exchange. This dual-channel engagement says, "I enjoy being physically connected to you even during ordinary conversation."

The hand contains numerous nerve endings, making it highly receptive to touch, yet playing with fingers remains comfortably in the realm of affection rather than explicitly sexual. This creates pleasurable sensation without pressure or expectation.

Phrase to Say

This gesture typically needs no verbal acknowledgment—

the touch speaks for itself while conversation continues on other topics.

Tips to Make It Work

Casualness: Keep the touch playful and light rather than intense or demanding, allowing it to complement rather than interrupt your conversation.

Awareness: Notice if he seems to welcome the contact or if he needs his hands free for expression or emphasis while speaking.

Variation: Alternate between different types of touch— holding, tracing, gentle pressure—rather than repetitive motion that might become distracting.

When to Use

This gesture creates lovely connection during casual conversations, while relaxing together, or during moments of storytelling or sharing. It's particularly effective during otherwise ordinary exchanges, elevating them through physical connection without redirecting their purpose.

planning an activity centred around his interests

WHY IT HELPS

Taking initiative to create an experience specifically tailored to his interests demonstrates both attentiveness and valuing of what brings him joy. When you plan an activity centred around something he loves—a visit to a specialty museum, tickets to a sporting event he follows, or an outing related to his hobbies—you're saying, "Your enjoyment matters enough for me to create space specifically designed for it."

What distinguishes this from casual participation is your proactive planning. Rather than merely accompanying him to his interests, you're actively creating the opportunity, showing that his passions are important enough to warrant your initiative and effort.

Phrase to Say

"I've arranged something I think you'll enjoy this weekend —it involves that pottery studio you mentioned wanting to visit." OR "I got us tickets to the classic car show on

Saturday—I know how much you appreciate vintage engines."

Tips to Make It Work

Observation: Base your planning on interests he's genuinely expressed rather than assumptions about what he should enjoy.

Balance: Focus on his enjoyment while ensuring the activity allows for shared experience rather than you merely observing his engagement.

Openness: Approach the experience with genuine curiosity about what he appreciates about this interest, allowing his enthusiasm to educate and expand your perspective.

When to Use

This gesture creates meaningful connection for birthdays or anniversaries, certainly, but carries even more impact when done for no particular occasion—transforming an ordinary day into evidence of ongoing attentiveness to what brings him joy.

twenty-four
warming his towel while he's in the shower

Anticipating comfort at a vulnerable transition point demonstrates both thoughtfulness and practical care. When you warm his towel while he's showering, you're creating an experience of being cared for precisely when we're at our most exposed. This nurturing gesture says, "I'm thinking about your comfort even when you're not present, and I want to extend the pleasure of your self-care routine."

What makes this particularly meaningful is how it addresses a moment of vulnerability with practical kindness. Emerging wet from a shower creates a brief period of discomfort before drying—your thoughtfulness transforms this transition into an unexpected moment of luxury and care.

Phrase to Say

"Your towel's warm and ready when you are." OR Simply

hand him the warmed towel with a smile, letting the gesture speak for itself.

Tips to Make It Work

Timing: Coordinate so the towel is warmed just before he finishes rather than cooling for several minutes.

Method: Use a towel warmer if you have one, briefly tumble the towel in a dryer, or even warm it against a radiator—the specific method matters less than the result.

Presentation: Hand it to him directly if appropriate, or place it within easy reach of the shower, making it immediately available when needed.

When to Use

This gesture creates beautiful care during ordinary morning routines, after he's been working outside in cold conditions, following exercise, or any time he's showering. Its unexpectedness during regular routines is what creates its impact, transforming mundane necessity into an experience of being thought about and cared for.

maintaining eye contact when he shares something meaningful

WHY IT HELPS

Undivided visual attention during vulnerable sharing creates a container of validation that many men rarely experience. When you maintain steady eye contact while he shares something meaningful—whether an accomplishment, concern, or personal reflection—you're offering full presence that acknowledges the significance of what's being expressed. This focused attention says, "What you're sharing deserves my complete engagement; I'm fully here with you in this moment."

What distinguishes this from casual listening is the deliberate quality of your attention. Rather than the divided awareness that characterises many interactions, your unwavering focus creates space where his words are received with the weight they deserve.

Phrase to Say

Your eyes communicate most powerfully here, but after

he's finished speaking, perhaps: "Thank you for sharing that with me." OR "I appreciate you telling me about this."

Tips to Make It Work

Quality: Maintain comfortable but unwavering eye contact —not a stare but steady focus that doesn't dart away during important points.

Patience: Resist the urge to fill pauses or silences, allowing him space to formulate thoughts without interruption.

Presence: Let your facial expressions respond naturally to what he's sharing, showing authentic engagement rather than neutral politeness.

When to Use

This gesture creates profound connection when he shares work achievements, childhood memories, current challenges, future hopes, or any subject he presents with particular care or vulnerability. It's especially valuable when he seems uncertain about whether his sharing is welcome or important—your focused attention confirms that it is indeed both.

reaching for his hand in a crowded space

WHY IT HELPS

In bustling environments where individual identity can feel diminished, physical connection creates an island of belonging. When you reach for his hand amid crowds, you're establishing a tangible link that distinguishes your relationship from the surrounding anonymity. This deliberate connection says, "Among all these people, you are my person. I choose connection with you specifically."

What makes this gesture particularly meaningful is its public nature. Unlike private affection, holding hands in crowded spaces communicates both connection and subtle pride in that connection—acknowledgment that your bond deserves external expression. For many men, this public claiming feels deeply affirming.

Phrase to Say

This gesture often speaks most eloquently without words —the reaching itself communicates everything necessary. If you speak at all, perhaps just a warm "There you are" as your hands connect.

Tips to Make It Work

Initiation: Reach with quiet confidence rather than hesitation, making the gesture feel natural and expected.

Grip: Find the right pressure—firm enough to feel secure in the crowd but gentle enough to remain comfortable.

Duration: Maintain the connection for meaningful periods rather than momentary contact, allowing it to ground both of you amid the stimulation of crowded environments.

When to Use

This gesture creates beautiful connection in shopping centres, busy streets, festivals, concerts, or any environment where physical proximity to others might otherwise create a sense of disconnection between you. It's particularly effective during transitions between spaces or activities, creating continuity of connection amid changing surroundings.

twenty-seven
resting your hand on his thigh during a meal

WHY IT HELPS

Touch during shared activities creates a dual-layer experience of connection. When you rest your hand on his thigh during a meal, you're establishing physical intimacy alongside the social engagement of dining. This tactile connection says, "Even as we participate in this activity, I remain aware of you as my partner, not just my companion."

The thigh represents intimate but non-intrusive territory—more personal than touching an arm but not explicitly sexual like higher placement would suggest. This middle-ground connection acknowledges your physical bond while remaining appropriate for public or shared settings.

Phrase to Say

This gesture typically needs no verbal accompaniment—the touch speaks for itself while conversation focuses on other topics.

Tips to Make It Work

Placement: Rest your hand on the outer or top thigh, avoiding the inner thigh which carries more intimate implications.

Pressure: Keep your touch light but definite—present enough to be felt as intentional but not so heavy as to be distracting.

Naturalness: Let your hand rest in a way that feels comfortable for extended periods rather than creating a position you can only briefly maintain.

When to Use

This gesture creates lovely connection during meals at home or restaurants, while sitting together at social gatherings, or during any seated conversation. It's particularly effective during otherwise ordinary interactions, elevating them through physical connection without redirecting their purpose.

twenty-eight
standing close enough that your bodies touch slightly

WHY IT HELPS

Subtle physical proximity signals preference and intention without demanding attention. When you position yourself close enough that your bodies maintain slight contact—shoulders brushing, arms touching, hips occasionally meeting—you're creating a continuous current of connection beneath whatever else is happening. This deliberate closeness says, "I choose to be in your physical space. Your proximity is my preference, not just my circumstance."

Unlike more obvious gestures that might interrupt activity or conversation, this subtle positioning creates background awareness of connection that enhances rather than diverts from the primary experience. It's intimacy as accompaniment rather than focus.

Phrase to Say

This gesture requires no words—the proximity itself communicates everything necessary.

Tips to Make It Work

Subtlety: Create contact that feels natural and unforced rather than obvious or performative—the power lies in its seeming casualness.

Consistency: Maintain or repeatedly return to this proximity rather than briefly establishing and abandoning it, creating a reliable undercurrent of connection.

Adaptation: Adjust to his positioning while still maintaining your intention for contact, allowing the touch to feel mutual rather than imposed.

When to Use

This gesture creates beautiful connection while standing in queues, preparing meals together, attending social gatherings, or during any activity where you naturally stand near each other. It's particularly effective during otherwise functional activities, transforming practical proximity into chosen connection.

twenty-nine
tracing patterns on his back absentmindedly

Gentle, seemingly unconscious touch communicates comfort and ongoing connection without demanding response. When you trace patterns on his back while engaged in other activities—watching television, talking with friends, or reading beside each other—you're creating physical connection that enhances without interrupting. This casual contact says, "Touching you is my natural state. My hands find you even when my mind is elsewhere."

What distinguishes this from more deliberate touch is its quality of comfortable familiarity. Like the way we might absentmindedly stroke a beloved pet, this touch suggests deep comfort with physical connection—touch that happens not as special occasion but as natural expression of ongoing bond.

Phrase to Say

This gesture typically needs no verbal acknowledgment—

the touch exists as background to whatever conversation or activity is already happening.

Tips to Make It Work

Lightness: Keep your touch gentle enough to feel pleasant rather than distracting—this is enhancing background rather than demanding foreground attention.

Variation: Allow your patterns to change organically rather than repetitive motions that might become monotonous or irritating.

Authenticity: While described as "absentminded," ensure the touch comes from genuine desire for connection rather than performed distraction.

When to Use

This gesture creates lovely connection during relaxed time together—while watching television, during casual conversations with others, or in any setting where you're physically close but engaged in other activities. It's particularly effective during group settings, creating private connection amid shared experience.

thirty
asking about his day with genuine interest

Authentic curiosity about daily experience acknowledges the full person beyond roles or functions. When you ask about his day with genuine interest—not as perfunctory greeting but as sincere desire to understand his experience—you're creating space for him to exist as complex individual rather than provider, partner, or resource. This attentive inquiry says, "Your internal experience matters to me, not just what you accomplish or provide."

What elevates this beyond social convention is quality of attention. Unlike the automatic "How was your day?" that often expects the generic "Fine," your genuine interest invites real sharing, creating opportunity for connection through authentic exchange rather than scripted interaction.

Phrase to Say

"What was your day like?" OR "Tell me about something interesting that happened today." Follow-up questions based on his response show you're actually listening rather than just performing interest.

Tips to Make It Work

Timing: Choose moments when you both have capacity for actual conversation rather than when either of you is rushed or distracted.

Listening: Respond to what he actually shares rather than waiting for predetermined topics or directing toward what you think should matter.

Patience: Some men need time to transition from doing to sharing—allow space for his experience to unfold rather than expecting immediate depth.

When to Use

This gesture creates meaningful connection during evening transitions from work to home, during meals together, or any regular point where you reconnect after separation. It's particularly valuable when established as consistent practice rather than occasional inquiry, creating reliable space for sharing that builds trust over time.

"To be fully seen by somebody, then, and be loved anyhow-this is a human offering that can border on miraculous." - Elizabeth Gilbert

These gestures are about truly seeing him—asking him to teach you his passions, playing with his fingers while talking, remembering the small details he mentions in passing. When you stroke the back of his neck while he's driving or ask about his day with genuine interest, you're offering something miraculous: complete attention without judgment. You're saying, "I see who you are—your interests, your stress, your daily reality—and I choose to engage with all of it." This kind of witnessing creates safety for him to be fully himself, knowing he's not just tolerated but genuinely appreciated in his entirety.

creating a playlist of songs that remind you of him

WHY IT HELPS

Music creates emotional landscapes that words often can't express. When you curate a playlist specifically of songs that remind you of him or your relationship, you're mapping your emotional connection through another medium. This thoughtful gesture says, "You exist in my mind even when we're apart. These songs create a bridge between us across time and space."

What makes this particularly meaningful is its evidence of private thought. Unlike gifts purchased in the moment, a carefully considered playlist demonstrates ongoing awareness—moments when songs triggered thoughts of him, connections you noticed and preserved. It's tangible proof of his presence in your consciousness.

Phrase to Say

"I made you a playlist of songs that make me think of you. This one reminds me of our trip to the coast..." OR "I've been collecting songs that capture different aspects of what you mean to me. Would you like to listen together?"

Tips to Make It Work

Personalisation: Choose songs that connect specifically to your relationship—shared memories, inside jokes, qualities you appreciate—rather than generic romantic tracks.

Variety: Include different emotional tones that reflect the full spectrum of your connection, not just the obviously romantic moments.

Context: When sharing, briefly explain the connections you've made, allowing him to experience not just the music but your thought process in selecting it.

When to Use

This gesture creates beautiful connection as an unexpected gift on ordinary days, during long separations when you want to maintain closeness, or to commemorate relationship milestones. It's particularly meaningful when shared during activities where you can experience it together—road trips, quiet evenings at home, or any setting where music can envelop your shared space.

giving him space when he needs it

Why It Helps

Respecting natural rhythms of connection and solitude demonstrates profound understanding. When you recognise his need for space and provide it willingly—without resentment, constant checking, or emotional withdrawal—you're honouring his process while maintaining security in your bond. This respectful distance says, "I trust our connection enough to allow temporary separation. Your individual needs matter alongside our togetherness."

What distinguishes this from passive disconnection is its active, conscious quality. You're not simply absent but deliberately creating space while maintaining the underlying assurance of your continued presence. This difference transforms potential rejection into expression of genuine care.

Phrase to Say

"Take whatever time you need—I'll be here when you're ready." OR "It seems like you might need some space right now. Would that help?"

Tips to Make It Work

Authenticity: Ensure your offer comes from genuine understanding rather than passive-aggressive withdrawal or testing.

Clarity: Establish basic expectations about the separation —approximate duration, whether minimal contact is welcome—so it feels contained rather than unlimited.

Security: Provide reassurance of your continued presence and the relationship's stability while respecting his need for temporary separateness.

When to Use

This gesture creates meaningful support during periods of work intensity, when he's processing difficult emotions, after significant life events requiring internal integration, or simply during his natural cycles of needing solitude. It's particularly valuable when offered before he must explicitly request it, showing attunement to his needs even before they're articulated.

sliding your arm around his waist from behind

WHY IT HELPS

Embracing from behind creates a unique combination of affection and respect for autonomy. When you slide your arm around his waist while he's engaged in an activity—cooking, looking out a window, working on a project—you're connecting without redirecting, adding your presence to his experience without interrupting it. This considerate gesture says, "I want to be close to you without requiring you to shift your attention or activity."

The waist represents a particularly effective point of connection—intimate enough to feel personal but neutral enough to be comfortable in various contexts. Your arm encircling this area creates gentle containment that most men find both pleasurable and respectful.

Phrase to Say

This gesture often works best without words, letting the physical connection speak for itself. If you speak at all, perhaps a soft "Mmm" of appreciation for the contact or a simple "Hi there."

Tips to Make It Work

Approach: Move gently into his space, allowing your presence to register before the full embrace to avoid startling him.

Pressure: Find the right tension in your arm—firm enough to feel intentional but gentle enough to maintain comfort for both of you.

Duration: Allow the embrace to last long enough to register as meaningful connection rather than passing acknowledgment, giving time for him to relax into the contact.

When to Use

This gesture creates lovely connection while he's engaged in household activities, during momentary pauses in his projects, or anytime he's stationary but occupied. It's particularly effective when he's focused on tasks requiring concentration, offering connection that supports rather than diverts his attention.

thirty-four
planning a surprise that you know he'll genuinely enjoy

WHY IT HELPS

Thoughtfully designed surprises demonstrate both intimate knowledge and willingness to create joy. When you plan an experience specifically calibrated to his authentic preferences—not what you think he should want or what would make a good social media post—you're showing that you truly see him as an individual. This personalised effort says, "I pay such close attention to what brings you happiness that I can create experiences designed specifically for your enjoyment."

What distinguishes meaningful surprises from generic ones is their grounding in genuine observation rather than assumption. A surprise that truly fits his nature and preferences shows you've been paying attention to the real person, not just your idea of who he is or should be.

Phrase to Say

"I've arranged something I think you'll enjoy—just trust me with Saturday afternoon." OR "Remember how you mentioned wanting to try that new climbing gym? I've set up something there for us this weekend."

Tips to Make It Work

Authenticity: Base your surprise on preferences he's genuinely expressed or demonstrated rather than conventional ideas about what men should enjoy.

Scale: Match the surprise to your relationship context— sometimes small, thoughtful surprises create more connection than grand gestures that might create pressure.

Flexibility: Build in room for adaptation if needed, ensuring the experience feels like a gift rather than an obligation.

When to Use

This gesture creates meaningful connection for birthdays or anniversaries, certainly, but carries particular impact when done for no special occasion—transforming an ordinary day into evidence of ongoing thoughtfulness and attention to what brings him joy.

letting him catch you watching him with appreciation

WHY IT HELPS

Being witnessed in moments of competence or focus creates powerful validation. When you allow him to catch you watching him with genuine appreciation—whether he's working with his hands, engaged in a skill, or simply existing in his natural state—you're offering a specific kind of recognition that many men rarely receive. This appreciative gaze says, "I find genuine pleasure in observing you being yourself. Your natural state is worthy of admiration."

Unlike compliments that can sometimes create self-consciousness, being caught in authentic appreciation allows him to experience your positive regard without immediately needing to respond to it. This creates space for him to actually receive the affirmation rather than deflecting or minimising it.

Phrase to Say

When your eyes meet, perhaps a simple "I like watching you work/move/think" or even just a warm smile that acknowledges being caught without apology.

Tips to Make It Work

Authenticity: Only do this when genuinely feeling appreciation—manufactured admiration is quickly detected and undermines trust.

Ease: When discovered, respond with comfortable acknowledgment rather than embarrassment or excessive explanation—this normalises your appreciation as natural and appropriate.

Specificity: If you do speak, mention the particular quality you were appreciating—his focus, competence, the way he moves—rather than general admiration.

When to Use

This gesture creates beautiful connection when he's engaged in activities where he demonstrates skill or natural grace—working on projects, participating in sports or hobbies, solving problems, or even just moving through the world in his unique way. It's particularly effective during ordinary moments rather than obvious achievements, showing you value his inherent qualities not just his accomplishments.

touching his chest briefly when sharing a moment

WHY IT HELPS

The chest houses the heart, making it both physically and symbolically significant. When you briefly touch his chest during a shared moment—whether laughing together, making a point in conversation, or expressing affection—you're creating connection that feels simultaneously casual and meaningful. This gesture says, "I'm drawn to your core, to the centre of you, not just to the social persona you present."

What distinguishes this from more habitual touches is its deliberate placement. Unlike brushing an arm or touching a hand, reaching for his chest creates a moment of targeted connection that most men experience as both affirming and pleasantly unexpected.

Phrase to Say

This touch often accompanies words related to the moment itself—accentuating a point in conversation, emphasising shared laughter, or punctuating an expression of care—rather than requiring its own verbal acknowledgment.

Tips to Make It Work

Lightness: Keep the touch brief and gentle—a moment of connection rather than extended contact that might interrupt the flow of interaction.

Placement: The sternum or upper chest area generally works best—personal enough to feel meaningful but not so intimate as to feel invasive.

Context: Let the touch emerge naturally from genuine moments rather than feeling predetermined or performed.

When to Use

This gesture creates lovely connection during conversations, shared laughter, expressions of support, or moments of sudden realisation. It's particularly effective during transitions—emphasising a point before moving on, marking a moment of understanding, or punctuating an insight with physical connection.

remembering small details he's mentioned in passing

WHY IT HELPS

Few things demonstrate genuine attention more clearly than recalling what might seem like inconsequential details. When you remember and reference something he mentioned casually—a childhood memory, preference for a specific food, name of a colleague he's mentioned once— you're showing that his words register as significant even when they're not presented as important. This attentive recall says, "I listen to you fully, not just to the headlines of your life but to the subtle details that make you who you are."

Unlike remembering obvious information or special occasions, recalling passing mentions requires genuine attentiveness. It can't be faked or performed for effect— either you were truly listening or you weren't.

Phrase to Say

"I picked up that particular tea you mentioned liking at your grandparents' house." OR "Wasn't Kevin the colleague who helped you with that difficult client last month? How did that situation resolve?"

Tips to Make It Work

Naturalness: Incorporate these recalled details into conversation casually rather than announcing them with fanfare that might create self-consciousness.

Accuracy: Ensure you've remembered correctly— misremembered details can suggest performative rather than authentic attention.

Relevance: Reference details when genuinely related to current context rather than forcing them into conversation to demonstrate your recall.

When to Use

This gesture creates meaningful connection in ongoing conversations, when making choices that affect him, or when opportunities naturally arise to show you've retained information he's shared. It's particularly powerful when some time has passed since the original mention, showing your attention spans beyond the immediate moment to create continuity of understanding.

thirty-eight
gently massaging his shoulders when you notice tension

Why It Helps

Physical tension often accumulates without conscious awareness, becoming background discomfort that affects mood and energy. When you notice and address this tension through touch, you're acknowledging his physical experience before he may even fully register it himself. This attentive care says, "I'm paying attention to your nonverbal cues and physical state, not just to what you explicitly express."

What makes this especially meaningful is its practical nature. Unlike symbolic gestures, a shoulder massage provides immediate tangible relief, creating a direct experience of being cared for in a way that addresses actual need rather than just signaling affection.

Phrase to Say

"You seem tense here—let me help with that for a moment." OR "Your shoulders are carrying so much tension right now," as you begin the gentle massage.

Tips to Make It Work

Observation: Watch for subtle signs of physical tension—raised shoulders, stiffened neck, reduced movement—rather than waiting for verbal complaints.

Technique: Use firm but gentle pressure with thumbs along the trapezius muscle (the diagonal muscle connecting neck to shoulders) while supporting with your fingers.

Duration: Even a brief 30-60 second massage can provide significant relief and connection—it doesn't need to be an extended session to be effective.

When to Use

This gesture creates beautiful support after demanding workdays, during stressful periods, while he's focused on challenging tasks, or whenever you observe physical manifestations of tension. It's particularly effective when offered without being requested, showing attunement to his physical state before he has to articulate discomfort.

expressing genuine gratitude for something specific he does

Why It Helps

Appreciation that focuses on specific actions rather than general qualities creates powerful validation. When you express genuine gratitude for particular things he does—whether significant contributions or small habitual kindnesses—you're acknowledging both the action itself and the intention behind it. This specific recognition says, "I notice and value not just the outcome of your efforts but the care and thought they represent."

Unlike general statements like "You're so helpful," specific gratitude demonstrates actual observation and prevents appreciation from becoming generic or routine. It creates detailed evidence of being seen rather than generally approved of.

Phrase to Say

"The way you always make sure my car has petrol before long trips makes me feel so cared for—thank you for that thoughtfulness." OR "I really appreciate how you took time

to explain that technical issue to my father yesterday—
your patience made him feel respected."

Tips to Make It Work

Specificity: Identify exactly what action or behaviour
you're grateful for rather than making sweeping statements
about his helpfulness or kindness.

Impact: Express how his specific action affected you
emotionally or practically, connecting his behaviour to its
meaningful outcome.

Timing: Offer this appreciation close enough to the action
to feel relevant but not so immediately that it seems
automatic.

When to Use

This gesture creates meaningful acknowledgment after
you've benefited from his efforts, when you notice patterns
of care he consistently demonstrates, or when you reflect
on aspects of your relationship you particularly value. It's
especially powerful for actions he might consider routine or
unremarkable, highlighting significance he may not
recognise in his own behaviour.

complimenting a quality about him that you don't praise enough

WHY IT HELPS

Everyone is wonderfully complex and multi-faceted, yet we often receive recognition for only our most obvious traits. When you deliberately compliment an aspect of him that doesn't typically receive acknowledgment—perhaps his patience with children, aesthetic sensibilities, emotional perceptiveness, or intellectual curiosity—you're expanding his sense of being seen beyond his primary identity. This broadened recognition says, "I see the fullness of who you are, not just the parts that are most visible or obviously valuable."

What makes this particularly meaningful is how it addresses the common male experience of being recognised primarily for strength, competence, or provision while other qualities remain unacknowledged. Your specific appreciation of these less-celebrated traits creates space for his full humanity.

Phrase to Say

"I was watching you explain that complex idea at dinner last night, and your intellectual curiosity is so attractive—the way you explore concepts deeply rather than settling for easy answers." OR "I notice how carefully you choose your words when something matters—your verbal precision is a quality I really admire but probably don't mention enough."

Tips to Make It Work

Genuineness: Focus on qualities you authentically appreciate rather than strategically praising what you think should be acknowledged.

Speci!city: Identify not just the quality but how it manifests in observable behaviour, grounding your appreciation in actual experience rather than abstract attribution.

Freshness: Look for traits that feel underacknowledged rather than aspects of him that regularly receive positive attention.

When to Use

This gesture creates meaningful validation after you observe the quality in action, during reflective moments about your relationship, or when deliberately considering what you most value about him beyond the obvious. It's particularly powerful when offered during ordinary interaction rather than special occasions, showing these recognitions emerge from ongoing attention rather than ceremonial appreciation.

"The simple act of paying attention can take you a long way." - Keanu Reeves

Nolan Collins

Gestures 31-40 are fundamentally about the transformative power of attention. Whether you're creating playlists that show you think of him when apart or letting him catch you watching him with appreciation, these aren't dramatic declarations but quiet acts of awareness. In a world where most people feel invisible in their daily existence, your consistent attention becomes a profound form of love that reminds him someone is genuinely paying attention to who he is.

running your fingers along his forearm while sitting together

WHY IT HELPS

The forearm contains a unique combination of strength and sensitivity, making it particularly receptive to deliberate touch. When you slowly run your fingers along this area while sitting together, you're creating sensory pleasure that remains comfortably in the realm of affection rather than explicit sexuality. This gentle exploration says, "I take pleasure in the simple physicality of you, in touch that exists for connection rather than escalation."

Unlike more habitual or practical touches, this deliberate caress acknowledges his body as a source of pleasure in itself—not for what it does or provides but simply for how it feels beneath your fingers. This kind of appreciation is something many men rarely experience.

Phrase to Say

This gesture often works best without words, letting the sensation speak for itself. If anything, perhaps a contented sigh or soft "I love touching you" if the moment feels right for verbal affirmation.

Tips to Make It Work

Lightness: Keep your touch gentle but definite—firm enough to create clear sensation but light enough to stimulate nerve endings pleasurably.

Pace: Move slowly enough that the touch feels deliberate and appreciative rather than absent-minded or rushed.

Attention: Bring genuine focus to the sensation for both of you—this isn't background touching but a moment of intentional physical connection.

When to Use

This gesture creates lovely connection during quiet moments together—while watching television, during conversation, or in comfortable silences. It's particularly effective during otherwise ordinary interactions, elevating them through deliberate sensory pleasure without demanding response or escalation.

reaching out to touch him just because you want to

WHY IT HELPS

Spontaneous, desire-driven touch communicates genuine attraction beyond routine or obligation. When you reach out to touch him simply because you feel drawn to physical connection—brushing his arm as you pass, briefly resting your hand on his back, touching his face without prompt or purpose—you're demonstrating that physical connection with him remains an active desire rather than habitual behaviour. This spontaneous contact says, "My attraction to you isn't based on circumstance or expectation—it arises naturally from genuine desire for connection."

What distinguishes this from other touches is its lack of practical purpose or social convention. You're not touching to get attention, assist with a task, or fulfill relationship expectations—you're touching purely because something in you wants that physical connection in that moment.

Phrase to Say

If words accompany this touch at all, they might be as simple as "I just wanted to touch you" or a soft "Mmm" of appreciation. Often, the most powerful approach is letting the gesture speak entirely for itself.

Tips to Make It Work

Authenticity: Only reach out when genuinely feeling the impulse rather than performing spontaneity—the authentic quality of desire-driven touch is what creates its impact.

Variety: Allow these touches to vary naturally in location, duration, and quality rather than falling into predictable patterns that might feel routine.

Attunement: Notice his response to different types of spontaneous touch, developing awareness of what registers most positively for him.

When to Use

This gesture creates beautiful connection throughout daily life—while passing in hallways, during parallel activities in shared space, in brief moments of proximity during otherwise separate tasks. Its power lies precisely in its independence from special occasions or designated connection times, emerging instead from genuine impulses throughout ordinary interaction.

forty-three
telling him the specific impact his actions have on you

Men often evaluate themselves based on the tangible effects of their actions rather than intentions or efforts alone. When you explicitly connect his specific behaviours to their meaningful impact on your experience, you're providing the exact kind of feedback that registers most powerfully. This clear connection says, "What you do matters in specific, observable ways. Your actions create real difference in my life."

Unlike general appreciation, impact-focused feedback creates direct evidence of effectiveness. It transforms abstract concepts like "being supportive" into concrete realities like "when you listened without trying to solve my work problem yesterday, I felt truly heard and could think more clearly afterward."

Phrase to Say

"When you call to check in during your lunch break, it makes me feel prioritised even during your busy day." OR

"The way you remembered to get that specific ingredient I love for dinner tonight makes me feel so seen and valued."

Tips to Make It Work

Specificity: Identify the exact action that had impact rather than general patterns or qualities.

Personal Effect: Express the concrete difference his action made in your emotional or practical experience rather than objective outcomes.

Timeliness: Share this reflection close enough to the action to feel connected but not so immediately that it seems automatic or conditional.

When to Use

This gesture creates meaningful acknowledgment after specific actions that positively affected you, during reflective conversations about your relationship, or when you notice patterns of behaviour that consistently enhance your experience. It's particularly effective for actions he might consider small or unremarkable, highlighting significance he may not recognise in his own contributions.

forty-four
tucking notes in unexpected places for him to find

Surprise affirmation creates evidence of being thought about beyond direct interaction. When you tuck notes expressing appreciation, desire, or loving thoughts in places he'll discover later—his laptop bag, wallet, jacket pocket, work lunch—you're extending your connection across time and space. This thoughtful gesture says, "You exist in my mind and heart even when we're not together. I create moments of connection for you to discover when I'm not present."

What makes unexpected notes particularly meaningful is their demonstration of forethought. Unlike spontaneous expressions, these require planning and intention, showing that your appreciation isn't merely responsive to his presence but active even in his absence.

Phrase to Write

"Thinking about how your calm helped us through that challenge last week. You're my rock." OR "The way you looked this morning stayed with me all day. You take my breath away without even trying."

Tips to Make It Work

Personalisation: Write messages that connect to specific aspects of your relationship rather than generic sentiments that could apply to anyone.

Discretion: For notes placed in work contexts, ensure the content respects appropriate boundaries while still feeling meaningful.

Surprise: Place notes where they'll be genuinely unexpected rather than in obvious locations, creating moments of discovery rather than anticipated findings.

When to Use

This gesture creates lovely connection before trips apart, during particularly demanding periods when direct interaction might be limited, or simply as ongoing practice during ordinary time together. Its power lies in unpredictability—not a routine communication but surprise affirmation that punctuates daily life with evidence of being held in mind.

forty-five
giving him your full attention when he's speaking

Why It Helps

Undistracted presence has become increasingly rare and correspondingly valuable. When you put down your phone, turn away from screens, pause what you're doing, and give him your complete attention while he speaks—whether about his day, a problem, or a passion—you're offering one of the most profound forms of respect. This focused presence says, "What you have to say matters enough for me to temporarily set aside everything else. You have my full being, not just partial awareness."

Unlike divided attention that characterises many interactions, your deliberate focus creates space where his thoughts and feelings can be expressed without competing with other demands. This kind of attentiveness is particularly meaningful for men who often experience being listened to primarily for information or solutions rather than for connection.

Phrase to Say

What matters most is what you don't say—not interrupting, completing thoughts, or redirecting to your experience. If speaking, perhaps: "Tell me more about that," or "I'd like to understand better," encouraging deeper sharing.

Tips to Make It Work

Physical Signals: Turn your body toward him, maintain comfortable eye contact, and provide nonverbal feedback (nodding, responsive expressions) that shows engagement.

Devices: Put phones completely away rather than just face-down, and turn off screens or move away from them if possible.

Patience: Allow his thoughts to unfold at their natural pace without rushing to conclusions or solutions, creating space for his complete expression.

When to Use

This gesture creates profound connection when he's processing challenges, sharing accomplishments, expressing confusion or uncertainty, or simply relating ordinary experiences from his day. It's particularly valuable when applied to topics he cares about but might consider uninteresting to others, showing that your attention responds to his enthusiasm rather than just objective importance.

forty-six
stroking the back of his neck while he's driving

WHY IT HELPS

The nape of the neck represents a uniquely vulnerable yet accessible area, particularly when someone's focus is necessarily directed elsewhere. When you gently stroke this area while he's driving, you're creating pleasurable connection that acknowledges his physical presence without demanding a shift in his primary attention. This thoughtful touch says, "I can appreciate and connect with you even while you're engaged in other necessary tasks."

What distinguishes this from more casual contact is its placement on a seldom-touched area rich with nerve endings. The back of the neck responds sensitively to gentle touch, creating significant pleasure from minimal contact —perfect for situations where more extensive interaction isn't appropriate.

Phrase to Say

This gesture typically works best without words, letting the sensation speak for itself while he maintains driving focus.

If anything, perhaps a soft "Mmm" or "I like touching you here" if conversation already flows naturally.

Tips to Make It Work

Gentleness: Keep your touch light and steady—this area responds best to consistent, gentle contact rather than varied pressure.

Placement: Focus on the hairline and upper neck area rather than the sides which might be ticklish or distracting.

Duration: Maintain the contact long enough to register as deliberate connection rather than casual touch, allowing time for the sensation to fully register.

When to Use

This gesture creates lovely connection during car journeys of any length, particularly when conversation naturally lulls or when traffic demands his full attention. It's especially effective during otherwise routine drives, transforming functional travel into an opportunity for quiet intimacy without distraction.

sending him a message that hints at your desire for him

WHY IT HELPS

Explicit appreciation of your physical attraction creates powerful affirmation. When you send a message that hints at your desire—not necessarily overtly sexual but clearly indicating physical attraction—you're acknowledging an aspect of your connection that men often feel uncertain about. This expressive message says, "My attraction to you remains active and intentional, not just habitual or historical."

What makes this particularly meaningful is its deliberate nature. Unlike responding to initiated intimacy, proactively expressing desire shows that your attraction exists independently, arising from your own internal response to him rather than mere reciprocation.

Phrase to Say

"Just thinking about the way you looked in that blue shirt this morning... looking forward to seeing you later." OR

"That goodbye kiss is still on my mind. You have no idea what you do to me sometimes."

Tips to Make It Work

Personalisation: Reference specific aspects of him that genuinely spark desire rather than generic sensuality that could apply to anyone.

Suggestion: Create anticipation through hint and implication rather than explicit detail, allowing his imagination to engage with your expressed desire.

Timing: Send when you're apart but will reconnect relatively soon, creating pleasant anticipation rather than frustration.

When to Use

This gesture creates meaningful affirmation during workday separations, while either of you is travelling, or simply amid the routine rhythms of daily life. It's particularly effective during periods when physical intimacy might have become predictable or less frequent, reintroducing the element of desire and anticipation into your connection.

placing your hand over his heart and just feeling it beat

WHY IT HELPS

The heartbeat represents perhaps the most fundamental rhythm of existence—constant, life-sustaining, yet rarely acknowledged. When you place your hand over his heart and simply rest there, feeling its steady pulse, you're connecting with him at his most essential level. This intimate gesture says, "I appreciate you at your most basic humanity—this rhythm that has continued since before birth and symbolises your very existence."

Unlike more common forms of touch, this connection carries symbolic weight beyond physical sensation. You're literally feeling the organ culturally associated with emotion and life force, creating a moment of profound acknowledgment that transcends ordinary interaction.

Phrase to Say

This gesture often communicates most powerfully through silence, letting the physical connection speak for itself. If words feel appropriate, perhaps a quiet "I love feeling your heart" or simply "There you are."

Tips to Make It Work

Stillness: Allow your hand to rest quietly rather than moving or stroking, creating space to actually feel the heartbeat rather than just touching the area.

Presence: Bring your full attention to the sensation, noticing the strength and rhythm unique to him rather than touching absent-mindedly.

Duration: Give the moment time to develop fully—it often takes several seconds of contact before the heartbeat becomes clearly perceptible through clothing and tissue.

When to Use

This gesture creates profound connection during quiet intimate moments—while embracing, during peaceful conversation, before sleep, or upon waking. It's particularly meaningful during ordinary times rather than only during heightened emotion, showing that you value his fundamental existence not just his peak experiences.

showing enthusiasm about something he's excited about

WHY IT HELPS

Shared enthusiasm creates validation beyond mere tolerance or polite interest. When you respond with genuine excitement to something that animates him— whether a hobby, achievement, idea, or plan—you're affirming not just the specific topic but his right to experience and express passion. This energetic engagement says, "Your enthusiasm is worthwhile and contagious. What excites you matters enough to affect my emotional state too."

Unlike passive acceptance or dutiful attention, authentic shared excitement creates true resonance. It transforms his interest from something he pursues separately or apologetically into terrain for mutual engagement and pleasure.

Phrase to Say

"Tell me more about how that works—the way you describe it makes it sound fascinating." OR "I love seeing you so lit up about this project—your energy is contagious."

Tips to Make It Work

Authenticity: Find genuine points of interest within his enthusiasm rather than manufacturing excitement you don't feel—specific curiosity often evolves naturally into broader engagement.

Questions: Ask questions that reflect actual interest and help you understand what specifically excites him about the subject.

Engagement: Follow up later about the topic rather than containing your interest to the initial conversation, showing it has registered as meaningful rather than momentary.

When to Use

This gesture creates meaningful connection when he shares new interests, accomplishments at work or in hobbies, creative ideas, or future plans. It's particularly powerful when applied to pursuits he might consider niche or potentially boring to others, showing that your interest responds to his enthusiasm rather than just inherent appeal of the subject.

fifty
surprising him with something aligned with his interests

WHY IT HELPS

Thoughtful surprises demonstrate ongoing attention and valuing of what brings him joy. When you present him with something specifically connected to his interests—a book by an author he enjoys, a tool related to his hobby, or tickets to an event in his field of passion—you're showing that you notice and remember what matters to him. This attentive gesture says, "I pay attention to what brings you pleasure and actively look for ways to contribute to your enjoyment of things you love."

Unlike generic gifts, interest-aligned surprises demonstrate specific observation. They can't be selected through general knowledge of what men typically like but require particular attention to his unique preferences and passions.

Phrase to Say

"I saw this and immediately thought of your collection." OR "I remembered you mentioned wanting to explore this author's work, so I picked this up for you."

Tips to Make It Work

Specificity: Choose items or experiences that connect to particular aspects of his interest rather than general categories—not just any book about his hobby but one that addresses the specific elements he's mentioned.

Observation: Base your selection on preferences he's genuinely expressed or demonstrated rather than assumptions about what he should like within his interest area.

Presentation: Offer the surprise with simple acknowledgment rather than fanfare that might create pressure for proportionate gratitude.

When to Use

This gesture creates meaningful connection when you happen upon something perfectly suited to his interests, after he's mentioned wanting to explore a particular aspect of his hobby, or simply as an unexpected affirmation on an ordinary day. Its power lies in unpredictability—not an obligatory gift but tangible evidence that his passions remain present in your awareness even when not explicitly discussed.

"Love recognizes no
barriers. It jumps hurdles,
leaps fences, penetrates
walls to arrive at its
destination full of hope." -
Maya Angelou

These ten gestures reveal the beauty of giving without expectation—running your fingers along his forearm simply because you enjoy touching him, reaching out to connect just because you want to, giving him your full attention when he speaks. When you tell him the specific impact his actions have on you or tuck notes for him to find later, you're demonstrating that love leaps the barriers of routine and expectation to arrive at genuine connection. Your willingness to stroke the back of his neck while he's driving or send messages hinting at your desire shows love that refuses to be confined by circumstance, always finding ways to reach him with hope and appreciation.

initiating a passionate kiss without expectation of more

WHY IT HELPS

Physical passion that exists for its own sake creates powerful affirmation. When you initiate a deeply engaged kiss without suggestion or expectation that it will lead to more intimate contact, you're communicating that the kiss itself is meaningful and satisfying. This deliberate gesture says, "I desire this specific connection with you—not as a means to something else, but as a complete expression in itself."

What distinguishes this from routine affection or preliminary intimacy is its self-contained nature. A passionate kiss given without agenda validates physical connection as inherently valuable rather than merely functional or transitional. This counters the common male experience of physical affection being primarily valued as initiation rather than expression.

Phrase to Say

This gesture typically needs no verbal introduction—the kiss itself communicates everything necessary. Afterward, perhaps a soft "I just needed to kiss you like that" or simply a warm smile before returning to previous activities.

Tips to Make It Work

Presence: Bring your full attention and engagement to the kiss itself rather than dividing focus between current contact and potential escalation.

Intensity: Allow genuine passion to infuse the kiss—depth, duration, and physical response that communicates real desire rather than perfunctory contact.

Conclusion: End the kiss cleanly without apology or explanation, returning to previous activities naturally to emphasise its complete nature.

When to Use

This gesture creates powerful connection during otherwise ordinary moments—while preparing dinner, before leaving for work, during a brief passing in the hallway. Its unexpectedness during routine activities is what creates its impact, transforming functional proximity into momentary intensity without disrupting the day's natural flow.

fifty-two
holding his gaze a moment longer than necessary

WHY IT HELPS

Extended eye contact creates a distinct moment of chosen connection amid routine interaction. When you deliberately hold his gaze slightly longer than social convention dictates—not long enough to create discomfort but beyond casual acknowledgment—you're establishing an island of intimacy within ordinary exchange. This lingering connection says, "I'm not just looking at you out of habit or courtesy; I'm choosing to truly see you in this moment."

Unlike the constant eye contact of focused conversation, these briefly extended moments create punctuation in daily interaction—small but significant reminders of deeper connection beneath social routine. They acknowledge the private bond that exists regardless of context or company.

Phrase to Say

This gesture works most powerfully without words, letting the extended gaze speak for itself. Your eyes might hold a question, appreciation, desire, or simply recognition—the specific quality matters less than the deliberate extension of connection.

Tips to Make It Work

Authenticity: Allow genuine feeling to show in your eyes rather than maintaining a neutral or performative expression—the emotional quality transforms duration from awkward to intimate.

Duration: Extend just slightly beyond comfortable social convention—typically just 1-2 seconds longer than standard eye contact—creating significance without discomfort.

Conclusion: End with a small smile, subtle nod, or gentle shift away rather than abrupt breaking of contact, allowing the moment to resolve naturally.

When to Use

This gesture creates beautiful connection during everyday interactions—passing coffee across the table, concluding a routine conversation, saying goodbye before work, or greeting upon return. It's particularly effective during ordinary exchanges that might otherwise pass without emotional significance, infusing them with momentary depth that acknowledges the relationship beneath functional interaction.

nestling into him naturally when sitting together

WHY IT HELPS

Physical alignment that seeks closeness rather than merely sharing space demonstrates active preference. When you adjust your position to nestle against him while sitting together—shifting to rest against his side, laying your head on his shoulder, or aligning your body to maximise contact —you're creating physical evidence of desire for proximity. This deliberate positioning says, "Being physically close to you isn't just convenient or coincidental; it's my active preference and pleasure."

Unlike maintaining polite distance or accidental contact, intentionally creating alignment shows that physical connection remains a chosen priority rather than mere habit or obligation. It demonstrates that his physical presence continues to draw you in, even in an established relationship.

Phrase to Say

This gesture often needs no verbal acknowledgment—the physical positioning speaks for itself. If anything, perhaps a contented sigh or soft "You're comfortable" as you settle against him.

Tips to Make It Work

Naturalness: Allow the movement to seem relaxed and spontaneous rather than ceremonial or self-conscious, creating the sense that closeness is your natural inclination.

Comfort: Find positioning that genuinely feels good for extended contact rather than creating a pose that looks intimate but causes physical strain over time.

Responsiveness: Remain subtly attuned to his body language, adjusting if you sense tension or leaning further in if you feel welcome receptivity.

When to Use

This gesture creates lovely connection while watching television, reading together, sitting in public spaces, or during any shared sedentary activity. It's particularly effective during otherwise routine evenings or casual social settings, showing that proximity remains actively chosen even within established patterns rather than merely default positioning.

fifty-four
touching your collarbone in a sensual way when he's looking at you

Self-touch that acknowledges your own sensuality creates a particular kind of invitation to witness without demanding response. When you deliberately touch your collarbone in a slow, appreciative way while he's looking at you, you're creating visual connection to your physical self while maintaining complete autonomy. This self-assured gesture says, "I am comfortable in my sensuality and choose to share that awareness with you specifically."

Unlike more obvious or performative gestures, this subtle self-touch operates in the intriguing middle ground between casual movement and deliberate sensuality. It acknowledges physical attraction as an element of your connection without reducing the interaction to purely sexual territory.

Phrase to Say

This gesture typically works best without words, letting the visual communication stand alone. Your eyes might meet his during or after the touch, acknowledging shared awareness without verbal emphasis.

Tips to Make It Work

Subtlety: Keep the movement slow and deliberate but understated—tracing your collarbone lightly or resting fingertips there momentarily rather than dramatic flourish.

Authenticity: Ensure the gesture emerges from genuine comfort with your own physicality rather than performance for effect, allowing real sensuality to infuse the movement.

Timing: Choose moments when he's already looking at you rather than using the gesture to interrupt or redirect his attention, allowing it to deepen existing connection rather than demand new focus.

When to Use

This gesture creates intriguing connection during otherwise ordinary interactions—conversations across the dinner table, casual social gatherings, relaxed time at home. It's particularly effective amid otherwise nonsexual contexts, creating momentary acknowledgment of physical attraction as an ongoing undercurrent within your relationship even during periods focused on other aspects of connection.

fifty-five
letting your
fingertips linger
when passing
something to him

Brief moments of extended contact transform functional interaction into opportunity for connection. When you deliberately let your fingertips linger against his while passing an object—a coffee mug, document, TV remote, or any everyday item—you're creating a private moment of chosen touch within practical exchange. This intentional extension says, "Even routine interactions contain opportunities for meaningful contact between us."

Unlike incidental touching during transfers, allowing your fingers to maintain contact slightly longer than necessary creates distinct awareness of connection. It transforms automatic movement into chosen engagement, highlighting the relationship beneath functional interaction.

Phrase to Say

This gesture typically needs no verbal acknowledgment— the extended contact speaks for itself within the ordinary exchange of "Here you go" or "Thank you" that typically accompanies passing objects.

Tips to Make It Work

Subtlety: Extend contact just long enough to register as intentional rather than accidental—typically just 1-2 seconds longer than necessary transfer requires.

Attention: Bring momentary focus to the point of connection rather than treating it as background to the practical exchange, allowing shared awareness of the lingering touch.

Naturalness: Incorporate this extended contact smoothly within normal movement patterns rather than creating obvious or stilted delay that interrupts functional flow.

When to Use

This gesture creates lovely connection during everyday exchanges—passing morning coffee, handing over car keys, transferring tools or household items, sharing food or drinks. Its effectiveness lies in transforming dozens of otherwise automatic daily interactions into brief but meaningful moments of chosen connection, creating a day interwoven with intentional touch rather than isolated instances of affection.

playing with his hair while watching tv

WHY IT HELPS

Casual, sustained touch during shared activities creates connection without demanding attention. When you play with his hair while watching television—running your fingers through it, massaging his scalp lightly, or simply stroking in a gentle rhythm—you're providing physical pleasure that enhances rather than interrupts the primary experience. This ongoing touch says, "Our physical connection remains active even during ordinary activities; it doesn't require special occasions or focused attention."

The scalp contains thousands of nerve endings, making hair play particularly pleasurable for most people. Yet unlike more intimate forms of touch, this contact remains comfortably in the realm of affection that can be enjoyed without escalation or response requirement.

Phrase to Say

This gesture typically needs no verbal acknowledgment— the touch exists as pleasant background to whatever you're watching. If anything, perhaps a soft "Your hair feels nice" or "Is this relaxing?" if conversation naturally arises.

Tips to Make It Work

Gentleness: Keep movements slow and light, particularly at first—some people have sensitive scalps that respond better to very gentle touch rather than firmer pressure.

Consistency: Maintain the contact long enough to become genuinely relaxing rather than just momentary acknowledgment—sustained touch often takes several minutes to create its full soothing effect.

Attention: While your primary focus remains on the programme, bring enough awareness to your touch to maintain deliberate rather than absent-minded quality.

When to Use

This gesture creates lovely connection during relaxed evenings at home, while watching films or shows together, or during any extended sedentary activity. It's particularly effective during otherwise ordinary routines, transforming functional shared time into opportunity for ongoing physical pleasure without disrupting the primary experience.

fifty-seven
bringing up a happy memory you share unexpectedly

WHY IT HELPS

Shared history creates bonds that distinguish intimate relationship from all other connections. When you unexpectedly reference a specific happy memory you share —perhaps a travel moment, private joke, or meaningful conversation—you're acknowledging the unique landscape of experience that belongs only to you two. This thoughtful recall says, "Our history has created something valuable in my mind. These moments live on inside me even when we're not actively discussing them."

Unlike reminiscing during designated nostalgic occasions, spontaneous memory reference during ordinary time shows that your shared past remains actively present in your consciousness. It demonstrates that special moments aren't just filed away but continue influencing your inner experience.

Phrase to Say

"That sunset reminded me of the one we saw in Cornwall last summer—remember how the colours kept changing every few minutes?" OR "The way you just laughed sounded exactly like when that waiter spilled ice water in your lap at that fancy restaurant in Edinburgh."

Tips to Make It Work

Specificity: Reference particular details rather than general events, showing that you've retained the texture and nuance of the experience rather than just its broad outline.

Positivity: Focus on genuinely happy or meaningful memories rather than complicated ones that might carry mixed emotions, unless those complexities have been well-processed between you.

Casualness: Offer the memory naturally within conversation rather than with ceremony that might create pressure for proportionate response.

When to Use

This gesture creates beautiful connection during ordinary conversations, while engaged in everyday activities, or whenever a natural trigger reminds you of a shared experience. It's particularly effective during otherwise unremarkable moments, transforming routine interaction into opportunity for reconnection with your unique shared history.

fifty-eight
whispering something appreciative in his ear

Whispered words create immediate intimacy through both physical proximity and private communication. When you bring your lips close to his ear to share something appreciative—a compliment, expression of desire, or acknowledgment of a quality you value—you're creating a moment of exclusive connection regardless of context. This intimate approach says, "This message is for you alone, personal and private between us even amid other company or activities."

What distinguishes whispered appreciation from ordinary compliments is its deliberate privacy. Even in completely private settings, the whispered delivery creates a distinct quality of intimate disclosure that acknowledges the special nature of what's being expressed.

Phrase to Say

"The way you handled that situation showed such quiet strength—it's one of the things I most admire about you."

OR "I love watching you like this—you have no idea how attractive you are when you're completely in your element."

Tips to Make It Work

Proximity: Move close enough that your lips nearly touch his ear, creating both sensory pleasure from your breath and complete privacy for your words.

Specificity: Whisper something genuinely meaningful and particular to him rather than generic appreciation, using the intimate delivery to convey truly personal acknowledgment.

Timing: Choose moments when the whisper feels natural rather than ceremonial—perhaps amid background noise, during group settings, or as brief connection during parallel activities.

When to Use

This gesture creates powerful connection during social gatherings, public events, family activities, or any context where brief private communication creates contrast with surrounding circumstances. It's particularly effective when what you're expressing might embarrass him if overheard by others, creating safe space for vulnerability through absolute privacy.

fifty-nine
telling him you're proud of him immediately after an achievement

WHY IT HELPS

Timely recognition of effort and accomplishment creates powerful validation. When you explicitly tell him you're proud immediately after he's achieved something meaningful—whether professional success, personal growth, or handling a challenging situation well—you're providing affirmation during a uniquely receptive moment. This prompt acknowledgment says, "I see not just the outcome but the work, courage, or growth it represents, and I value who you are becoming through these achievements."

What makes immediate pride expressions particularly meaningful is their authentic spontaneity. Unlike carefully considered reflections shared later, immediate recognition captures genuine emotional response before analysis or perspective has reshaped the reaction, creating rare transparency about your unfiltered positive regard.

Phrase to Say

"I'm so proud of how you handled that difficult conversation—the way you stayed both firm and respectful showed real integrity." OR "Watching you achieve this after all the obstacles you've overcome makes me incredibly proud to be with you."

Tips to Make It Work

Specificity: Identify exactly what aspects of the achievement or behaviour prompt your pride rather than general congratulations.

Sincerity: Ensure your expression reflects genuine feeling rather than perfunctory acknowledgment—authentic emotion registers far more powerfully than dutiful praise.

Connection: Link your pride explicitly to who he is rather than just what he's done, highlighting character qualities that the achievement represents.

When to Use

This gesture creates meaningful validation after work achievements, handling challenging interactions well, completing personal projects, or showing growth in areas of previous struggle. While particularly powerful immediately following achievements, thoughtful expressions of pride about past accomplishments can be equally meaningful when they demonstrate reflection about the significance of something he may have considered ordinary or expected.

sixty

initiating simple brief physical touch throughout the day

WHY IT HELPS

Consistent physical connection during ordinary times demonstrates ongoing awareness and desire rather than compartmentalised affection. When you initiate simple, brief touches throughout your day together—a hand on the arm while passing, fingers brushing his back in the kitchen, briefly squeezing his shoulder while he works—you're creating a tapestry of physical connection that exists independently of designated intimate time. This ongoing contact says, "My awareness of you physically isn't limited to specific moments; it persists throughout our shared existence."

Unlike more significant gestures that might be saved for particular occasions, these brief touches create continuity of physical connection across contexts. They transform daily life from parallel existence occasionally interrupted by intimacy into constant low-level awareness of physical presence and appreciation.

Phrase to Say

These brief touches typically need no verbal accompaniment—they exist as natural expression within the flow of ordinary interaction rather than requiring attention or acknowledgment.

Tips to Make It Work

Naturalness: Incorporate these touches smoothly within normal activity patterns rather than interrupting flow or creating obvious ceremony around contact.

Variety: Allow different types of touch to emerge organically—brief squeezes, light strokes, momentary pressure—creating textured experience rather than repetitive contact.

Attunement: Notice which forms of casual touch seem most welcomed and appreciated, developing awareness of his particular preferences for ongoing physical connection.

When to Use

This gesture creates beautiful connection throughout shared daily life—while moving through the house together, during parallel activities in the same space, through transitions between tasks or settings. Its power lies in frequency and distribution rather than individual significance, creating a day interwoven with physical acknowledgment rather than isolated islands of connection amid functional separation.

The real act of marriage takes place in the heart, not in the ballroom or church or synagogue. It's a choice you make-not just on your wedding day, but over and over again.
— Barbara De Angelis

These ten gestures embody the daily choice to nurture connection—initiating passionate kisses without expectation, holding his gaze longer than necessary, nestling into him naturally when sitting together. When you play with his hair while watching TV or bring up happy memories unexpectedly, you're making the choice to prioritise your bond in ordinary moments. Your willingness to whisper appreciative words in his ear or tell him you're proud immediately after achievements shows that love isn't just a feeling but an active decision to keep choosing each other, day after day, in countless small but meaningful ways.

creating a moment of connection before saying goodbye

WHY IT HELPS

Partings, even brief ones, represent transitions that benefit from deliberate acknowledgment. When you create a specific moment of connection before saying goodbye—whether through intentional eye contact, a lingering touch, or a brief but genuine exchange—you're marking the separation as meaningful rather than merely functional. This thoughtful pause says, "Your presence matters enough that its temporary absence deserves recognition. Our connection continues even when we're physically apart."

Unlike rushed or automatic goodbyes, a deliberate moment of connection transforms potential disconnection into opportunity for affirmation. It creates closure for the current interaction while simultaneously affirming continuity of the underlying bond.

Phrase to Say

"I'll be thinking of you today." OR "I'll miss you until later," accompanied by physical connection that emphasises the sincerity of your words.

Tips to Make It Work

Presence: Pause whatever you're doing to create full engagement for this brief moment rather than multitasking through the goodbye.

Eye Contact: Establish genuine visual connection rather than distracted or glancing acknowledgment, creating momentary but complete focus on each other.

Touch: Incorporate physical contact appropriate to your relationship and context—a lingering kiss, extended hug, or meaningful hand squeeze that distinguishes this goodbye from casual partings.

When to Use

This gesture creates meaningful transitions for daily separations—leaving for work, parting after shared meals, separating for different activities, or any context where your paths will diverge temporarily. It's particularly effective when established as consistent practice rather than occasional ritual, creating reliable punctuation between togetherness and separation.

telling him you love him in unexpected moments

WHY IT HELPS

Love expressions offered outside conventional timing create powerful affirmation. When you say "I love you" in unexpected moments—during ordinary activities, amid mundane conversation, or in contexts without obvious romantic cues—you're demonstrating that your feeling exists independently of circumstance rather than being triggered only by traditional prompts. This spontaneous expression says, "My love for you isn't reserved for special occasions or responses; it's an ongoing presence in my consciousness that sometimes simply must be voiced."

Unlike reciprocal exchanges or routine declarations, unexpected expressions demonstrate active rather than reactive love. They show that your feeling arises from internal awareness rather than external expectation, validating its authenticity precisely through their unpredictability.

Phrase to Say

A simple "I love you" offered without preamble or explanation—the unexpectedness itself being what gives the familiar words their distinctive power in this context.

Tips to Make It Work

Spontaneity: Allow these expressions to emerge naturally from genuine feeling rather than scheduling or manufacturing them for effect.

Simplicity: Keep the expression straightforward rather than elaborate, allowing its unexpectedness rather than its eloquence to create impact.

Authenticity: Ensure the timing reflects actual waves of feeling rather than strategic deployment, preserving the genuine quality that gives these expressions their particular power.

When to Use

This gesture creates beautiful affirmation during mundane activities—while cooking dinner, working on separate projects in shared space, driving together, or engaged in household tasks. Its effectiveness lies precisely in its contrast with circumstance, transforming ordinary moments into opportunities for renewed awareness of your underlying emotional connection.

holding his face gently between your hands while speaking

WHY IT HELPS

Framing the face creates focus that elevates ordinary conversation to significant exchange. When you gently hold his face between your hands while sharing thoughts or feelings, you're creating physical emphasis that signals importance beyond the words themselves. This intentional framing says, "What I'm expressing deserves your complete attention. This moment between us matters enough for deliberate elevation."

Unlike most conversational gestures that might touch a hand or arm, face-holding creates unusual intimacy through both the vulnerability of the area and the natural focusing effect of framing the sensory centres. It transforms casual exchange into momentary ceremony without requiring elaborate preparation or setting.

Phrase to Say

The content varies with circumstance, but this gesture particularly elevates expressions of serious appreciation, important acknowledgments, or heartfelt reassurance—moments where emotional significance benefits from physical emphasis.

Tips to Make It Work

Gentleness: Hold his face with deliberate lightness—this is framing rather than controlling, invitation rather than demand.

Eye Contact: Maintain steady, direct gaze throughout the gesture, creating dual connection through both touch and visual engagement.

Timing: Reserve this gesture for genuinely meaningful exchanges rather than routine conversation, preserving its distinctiveness as signal of particular significance.

When to Use

This gesture creates powerful connection during important relationship conversations, expressions of particularly deep feeling, moments of emotional vulnerability, or times when you specifically want to ensure your words register beyond intellectual understanding. Its relatively rare quality makes it especially effective for distinguishing truly significant communication from everyday exchange.

lying with your head in his lap during relaxed moments

WHY IT HELPS

Physical positioning that creates both intimacy and trust demonstrates profound comfort. When you lie with your head in his lap during relaxed moments—while watching television, reading together, or simply talking—you're creating a configuration that simultaneously offers closeness and acknowledges his supportive role. This trusting position says, "I feel completely safe allowing myself to be physically vulnerable with you. Your presence is my chosen place of rest."

Unlike side-by-side positioning that maintains equal height and autonomy, this configuration creates deliberate yielding that most men experience as profound affirmation. It physically embodies trust in a way that deeply resonates with masculine identity without requiring explicit acknowledgment.

Phrase to Say

This gesture typically needs no verbal enhancement—the physical positioning speaks eloquently on its own. If anything, perhaps a contented "This is nice" or "You make a perfect pillow" as you settle in.

Tips to Make It Work

Comfort: Find positioning that genuinely feels sustainable rather than creating strain that limits duration—perhaps using an actual pillow on his lap to create proper neck alignment.

Naturalness: Allow this configuration to emerge without ceremony or announcement, settling into it as natural expression of comfort rather than orchestrated intimacy.

Engagement: Balance between completely relaxed surrender and occasional acknowledgments—perhaps reaching up to touch his face or squeeze his hand periodically—that affirm active connection rather than merely using him as furniture.

When to Use

This gesture creates beautiful connection during quiet evenings together, weekend relaxation time, or any context of unhurried togetherness. It's particularly effective during otherwise ordinary moments, transforming routine shared time into opportunity for distinctive physical connection that differs from both practical positioning and explicitly romantic configuration.

greeting him with a kiss that lasts just a bit longer than usual

WHY IT HELPS

Duration transforms routine affection into deliberate connection. When you greet him with a kiss that extends just beyond habitual length—not dramatically longer but noticeably more engaged than automatic contact—you're disrupting potential patterns of ritualised affection. This extended greeting says, "This isn't merely obligatory acknowledgment; I'm genuinely pleased to see you and choose to express that through prolonged connection."

Unlike entirely routine kisses that may become effectively invisible through repetition, slightly extended duration creates just enough disruption to register as chosen rather than automatic. This subtle difference returns consciousness to what might otherwise become purely habitual interaction.

Phrase to Say

The kiss itself communicates most powerfully here, though you might accompany it with a warm "Hello you" or "I'm glad you're home" that reinforces the genuine pleasure in reconnection.

Tips to Make It Work

Attention: Bring full presence to the greeting rather than kissing while distracted by other thoughts or activities—the quality of engagement matters as much as literal duration.

Extension: Prolong the kiss just enough to register as deliberate without creating awkwardness—typically just 2-3 seconds beyond your usual greeting length is sufficient to create distinction.

Variation: Occasionally vary the quality as well as duration—perhaps slightly deeper pressure, a gentle hand on his face, or a brief second kiss—preventing even this extended greeting from becoming its own fixed pattern.

When to Use

This gesture creates meaningful reconnection at natural transition points—greeting after work separation, welcoming home from travel, or morning acknowledgment after sleep. It's particularly effective when incorporated as occasional variation rather than consistent replacement, creating unpredictability that prevents even extended greetings from becoming routine.

asking about something he's working on with genuine interest

WHY IT HELPS

Projects and pursuits represent extensions of identity for many men. When you ask specific questions about his current work or project with genuine curiosity—seeking to understand rather than merely acknowledge—you're validating not just the activity but the values and priorities it represents. This interested enquiry says, "I see this pursuit as meaningful because it matters to you, and I want to understand this aspect of your world more fully."

Unlike general questions like "How's your project going?" that can be answered with minimal engagement, specific enquiries demonstrate actual attentiveness to particulars. They show you've been paying enough attention to ask informed questions, creating opportunity for him to share expertise or enthusiasm without feeling he's imposing it.

Phrase to Say

"How did you resolve that challenge with the client you mentioned last week?" OR "I noticed you trying a different approach with that woodworking project—what made you decide to change techniques?"

Tips to Make It Work

Specificity: Reference particular aspects or challenges he's previously mentioned rather than asking generic questions that suggest minimal prior attention.

Openness: Ask from genuine interest rather than obligation, maintaining curiosity about his response rather than waiting to redirect conversation.

Engagement: Respond to his answers with follow-up questions that show you're processing the information rather than simply allowing him to talk.

When to Use

This gesture creates meaningful validation during ordinary conversations, while he's actively engaged in the project, or when natural references to his work arise. It's particularly effective for pursuits he might consider technical or potentially uninteresting to others, showing that your interest responds to his engagement rather than inherent appeal of the subject.

sixty-seven
expressing how attractive you find him in specific terms

WHY IT HELPS

Physical appreciation that focuses on specifics rather than generalities creates powerful affirmation. When you express attraction in particular terms—noting specific physical attributes, movements, or expressions that you find appealing—you're validating not just generic attractiveness but aspects unique to him. This detailed appreciation says, "I'm drawn to you specifically, not to generic male attributes. I notice and value what makes your physicality distinctly yours."

Unlike general compliments like "You look handsome" that could apply to anyone, specific expressions demonstrate actual observation and preference. They create evidence of being seen rather than generically approved, addressing the common male experience of feeling physically interchangeable or categorically rather than individually attractive.

Phrase to Say

"The way the muscles in your forearms move when you work with your hands is incredibly attractive to me." OR "I love the way your eyes crinkle at the corners when you laugh—it's one of my favourite things to see."

Tips to Make It Work

Authenticity: Focus only on aspects you genuinely find attractive rather than what you think you should compliment or what conventional standards suggest.

Specificity: Identify particular attributes or movements rather than general appearance, showing you're actually paying attention to details others might miss.

Timing: Offer these appreciations when they naturally occur to you rather than on schedule, allowing genuine response to guide timing rather than obligation.

When to Use

This gesture creates meaningful affirmation when you notice particularly appealing aspects of his physicality, during ordinary activities where his movements or expressions trigger appreciation, or in quieter moments when observation feels natural rather than evaluative. It's particularly powerful for physical attributes he might feel insecure about or take for granted, providing fresh perspective on aspects he may view neutrally or negatively.

resting your hand on his knee during conversation

WHY IT HELPS

Physical anchoring during verbal exchange creates multi-channel connection. When you rest your hand on his knee during conversation—whether serious discussion or casual exchange—you're establishing physical continuity alongside verbal engagement. This dual connection says, "Our communication exists on multiple levels simultaneously. My attention to you is both intellectual and physical."

Unlike gestures that might interrupt or redirect conversation, this steady contact creates background connection that enhances rather than competes with verbal exchange. It grounds interaction in physical awareness without demanding that awareness become the focus, allowing multiple forms of intimacy to operate concurrently.

Phrase to Say

This physical connection typically needs no verbal acknowledgment—it exists as comfortable enhancement to whatever conversation is already happening.

Tips to Make It Work

Steadiness: Maintain relatively consistent contact rather than fidgety or distracted movement that might create disruption rather than grounding.

Pressure: Keep your touch light but definite—present enough to maintain conscious connection but not so heavy as to become distracting.

Placement: Position your hand on the top or outer knee area rather than the inner knee, creating personal connection without unnecessary intimacy that might shift focus from conversation.

When to Use

This gesture creates lovely connection during important conversations, casual catching-up, shared meals, car journeys, or any context where you're primarily engaged verbally. It's particularly effective during discussions that might otherwise remain purely intellectual, bringing physical awareness into what could potentially become disembodied exchange.

creating small rituals that are just between the two of you

WHY IT HELPS

Private customs establish relationship territory that exists nowhere else. When you create and maintain small rituals specific to your relationship—particular goodbye sequences, inside-joke exchanges, or unique greetings— you're developing exclusive cultural elements that differentiate your connection from all others. These private practices say, "We have created something unique that belongs only to us. Our bond has generated its own special customs and language."

Unlike following generic relationship scripts, private rituals demonstrate actual co-creation. They show that your particular dynamic has produced distinctive patterns rather than merely adopting conventional forms, validating the relationship as unique rather than categorical.

Phrase to Say

The specific language varies entirely based on your unique rituals—perhaps particular phrases that have acquired special meaning, deliberately exaggerated versions of ordinary exchanges, or nonsense words that reference shared experiences.

Tips to Make It Work

Authenticity: Allow rituals to develop organically from genuine interaction rather than manufacturing them through deliberate design.

Consistency: Maintain the patterns regularly enough to establish them as reliable customs without rigidity that might make them feel obligatory.

Evolution: Allow your private practices to develop and change over time, remaining responsive to new experiences rather than fixed in initial forms.

When to Use

This gesture creates beautiful connection through regular performance of your established rituals—at consistent transition points, during particular activities, or in specific contexts where the pattern has naturally developed. The power lies in reliability without rigidity, creating recognisable patterns that provide continuity while remaining fresh enough to generate continued pleasure.

squeezing his hand three times to say "i love you"

WHY IT HELPS

Physical codes create intimate communication that transcends both privacy boundaries and verbal limitations. When you establish and consistently use hand squeezes as private code—particularly the classic three squeezes for "I love you"—you're creating communication that can function across contexts where words might be inappropriate or insufficient. This tactile language says, "Our connection has developed its own form of expression that works even when conventional communication doesn't."

The three-squeeze pattern specifically carries both cultural resonance and practical functionality—short enough to be unmistakable while complex enough to be clearly intentional. It creates momentary but profound recognition of emotional connection without requiring verbal exchange or public demonstration.

Phrase to Say

The physical pattern itself constitutes the communication here, typically without verbal accompaniment that would duplicate its message.

Tips to Make It Work

Clarity: Make each squeeze distinct enough to be clearly countable rather than blending into continuous pressure.

Consistency: Use the same pattern reliably so it develops clear meaning rather than random or variable squeezes that might create confusion.

Context: Employ this code particularly in situations where verbal expression might be difficult, inappropriate, or simply less meaningful than tactile communication.

When to Use

This gesture creates intimate connection during public events where private verbal exchange might be challenging, in emotional moments where words feel inadequate, during situations requiring quiet, or simply as regular affirmation during hand-holding. Its power lies in combining absolute privacy with unmistakable clarity, creating communication that works across virtually any context where physical contact is possible.

BONUS

I personally use the two squeeze gesture with my parnter at times for "I'm here" as a reminder that she's not alone. When you do this with some consistency, he'll often pick up on it and start dong it himself. Don't be afraid to explain it too so he doesn't act clueless!

"Love is not just looking at each other, it's looking in the same direction." - Antoine de Saint-Exupéry

These ten gestures demonstrate the art of moving forward together—creating moments of connection before goodbyes, telling him you love him in unexpected moments, holding his face gently while speaking. When you lie with your head in his lap or ask about his work with genuine interest, you're not just admiring each other but building a shared vision of your relationship. Your willingness to express how attractive you find him or create small rituals between you shows that love flourishes when two people face life's journey together, supporting each other toward the same destination of deeper connection and mutual understanding.

spontaneously dancing with him in the kitchen

WHY IT HELPS

Unexpected playfulness creates powerful contrast with routine activities. When you spontaneously initiate dancing in the kitchen—taking his hand during cooking, meal preparation, or clean-up—you're transforming functional space into momentary playground. This playful disruption says, "Our connection transcends practical necessity. Even amid ordinary tasks, we can create moments of pure joy and physical harmony."

Unlike scheduled recreation, spontaneous dancing demonstrates willingness to prioritise connection over efficiency or routine. It shows capacity to find joy together in the midst of necessity rather than only during designated leisure, validating the relationship as a source of ongoing pleasure rather than a separate category of experience.

Phrase to Say

"Dance with me for a minute" accompanied by extended hand or simply moving into dance position without verbal invitation, letting physical initiation create its own invitation.

Tips to Make It Work

Spontaneity: Allow these moments to emerge organically from genuine impulse rather than scheduled performance, preserving the delightful unexpectedness that creates their impact.

Simplicity: Keep the dancing uncomplicated—swaying together, a simple twirl, or basic steps rather than elaborate choreography that might create self-consciousness.

Duration: Make it brief enough to feel like a joyful interlude rather than interruption—typically 30-60 seconds creates perfect balance between significance and practicality.

When to Use

This gesture creates beautiful connection during ordinary domestic activities—meal preparation, dish washing, putting away groceries, or any kitchen-centred task. Its effectiveness lies precisely in its contrast with context, transforming mundane necessity into unexpected celebration without requiring special occasion or elaborate preparation.

brushing lint or adjusting his collar with tender attention

WHY IT HELPS

Caretaking gestures demonstrate both attentiveness and ongoing investment. When you brush lint from his clothing or adjust his collar with gentle focus—small acts of appearance maintenance—you're showing both observation of detail and desire for his wellbeing. This nurturing attention says, "I notice the small things about you, and I care enough to make minor adjustments that contribute to your comfort or presentation."

Unlike more dramatic forms of care, these small adjustments acknowledge the texture of daily life—the minor imperfections and shifts that accumulate through ordinary movement. They show willingness to engage with real rather than idealised existence, validating the relationship as grounded in actual rather than performed experience.

Phrase to Say

"Let me fix this for you" or simply a warm smile as you make the adjustment, letting the gesture speak primarily through action rather than words.

Tips to Make It Work

Gentleness: Perform these adjustments with light touch rather than aggressive correction, creating experience of care rather than critique.

Focus: Bring genuine attention to the moment rather than absent-minded fixing, transforming functional adjustment into opportunity for brief but complete connection.

Permission: Approach with body language that allows space for refusal if he's not receptive to adjustment in that moment, respecting autonomy alongside offering care.

When to Use

This gesture creates thoughtful connection before leaving home together, when reuniting after separate activities, or simply when noticing minor disarray during ordinary interaction. Its effectiveness lies in demonstrating ongoing attentiveness to his physical presence and wellbeing even in smallest details, showing that your care operates at all scales rather than only during significant moments.

seventy-three
telling him specifically what you find sexy about him

WHY IT HELPS

Explicit sexual appreciation outside of intimate contexts creates powerful affirmation. When you specifically articulate what you find sexy about him—particular physical attributes, expressions, capabilities, or qualities—during ordinary settings, you're validating his desirability beyond designated intimate moments. This deliberate expression says, "My attraction to you isn't compartmentalised to bedroom contexts. Your sexual appeal registers in my awareness throughout our shared life."

Unlike general compliments or appreciation expressed only during intimacy, specific acknowledgment during ordinary time demonstrates ongoing rather than situational desire. It creates evidence that attraction remains active rather than dormant between intimate encounters, validating continuous rather than episodic sexual connection.

Phrase to Say

"The way you focus when you're solving a problem is incredibly sexy to me—that intense concentration and confidence really turns me on." OR "I find your hands so sexy—the strength in them when you work but gentleness when you touch me is such a turn-on."

Tips to Make It Work

Specificity: Identify particular attributes or qualities rather than general attractiveness, showing you're responding to him uniquely rather than generic male sexuality.

Genuineness: Express only what authentically registers as sexually appealing for you rather than what you think should be acknowledged or what conventional standards suggest.

Context: Choose moments where such expression feels natural rather than intrusive, allowing appreciation to enhance rather than interrupt ongoing interaction.

When to Use

This gesture creates meaningful affirmation during casual conversation, while observing him engaged in activities, or during relaxed time together. It's particularly effective when offered during otherwise nonsexual contexts, creating acknowledgment of continuous attraction that exists alongside rather than separate from daily life and interaction.

saying thank you for the little things he does every day

WHY IT HELPS

Acknowledgment of routine contributions prevents invisibility of consistent care. When you express specific gratitude for regular actions—making coffee, handling household tasks, maintaining the car, remembering preferences—you're validating efforts that might otherwise disappear into expected background. This attentive appreciation says, "I notice and value your consistent contributions, not just exceptional efforts. What you might consider ordinary still registers as meaningful to me."

Unlike appreciation reserved for special occasions or unusual assistance, routine acknowledgment demonstrates ongoing awareness rather than selective attention. It counters the common experience of reliable contributions becoming effectively invisible through consistency, ensuring that regularity doesn't diminish perceived value.

Phrase to Say

"Thank you for filling my car with petrol—it's such a relief to never worry about running low." OR "I really appreciate you handling the recycling every week without being asked. It makes a difference to me."

Tips to Make It Work

Specificity: Identify the particular action rather than general helpfulness, showing you're actually noticing individual contributions rather than acknowledging abstract support.

Freshness: Vary both the contributions you acknowledge and your expressions of gratitude, preventing appreciation itself from becoming formulaic or predictable.

Sincerity: Ensure your tone and eye contact reflect genuine feeling rather than perfunctory acknowledgment, differentiating meaningful recognition from social convention.

When to Use

This gesture creates meaningful validation following ordinary contributions, during natural conversation, or at transition points in daily routine. While particularly important for actions he performs consistently, it's equally valuable for small spontaneous kindnesses that might seem minor to him but register significantly in your experience.

seventy-five
smiling at him with unguarded affection

WHY IT HELPS

Genuine facial expression communicates on levels words often cannot reach.

When you allow yourself to smile at him with completely unguarded affection—not the social smile of pleasantry but the unfiltered expression of emotional connection—you're creating a moment of rare authenticity. This transparent expression says, "This is my true feeling, without performance or restraint. In this moment, you're seeing exactly what you mean to me."

Unlike controlled or partial expressions that maintain emotional barriers, an unguarded smile represents momentary surrender of protective filtering. It creates unusual vulnerability through its complete transparency, offering a glimpse of feeling too authentic to manage or modify.

Phrase to Say

This expression communicates most powerfully without words, letting the unfiltered emotional quality speak entirely through facial language.

Tips to Make It Work

Authenticity: Allow this expression to emerge only from genuine waves of feeling rather than manufacturing it for effect, preserving the unfiltered quality that creates its impact.

Fullness: Let the smile engage your entire face—eyes, cheeks, even posture—rather than remaining contained to lips alone, creating complete rather than partial expression.

Connection: Maintain eye contact during this expression rather than glancing away, allowing him to fully receive the communication rather than glimpse it partially.

When to Use

This gesture creates profound connection during ordinary moments when genuine waves of feeling naturally arise— perhaps watching him engaged in activity, during quiet togetherness, upon reuniting after separation, or simply when authentic appreciation spontaneously emerges. Its power lies precisely in its ordinariness of context contrasted with extraordinariness of emotional transparency, transforming mundane moments into opportunities for profound connection.

The Art of Loving First

Your fingertips trace paths only you can see—
The curve of his shoulder as he reads,
The way tension gathers at the base of his neck,
The quiet strength in hands that build
*   and mend*
But rarely receive the gift of gentle touch.

You speak languages he's forgotten he
*   understands—*
The dialect of appreciation freely given,
The syntax of desire without expectation,
The vocabulary of seeing him completely
When he's convinced there's little worth
*   witnessing.*

Some days your gestures will bounce off armour
He's worn so long he thinks it's skin.
Your compliments may meet deflection,
Your touches might feel unreturned,
Your attention seemingly unwelcome.

But love that chooses to see
What he cannot yet see in himself
Has a patience that outlasts his resistance,
A persistence that penetrates walls
Built from years of feeling unseen.

You are teaching him a new language—
That he deserves touch without transaction,
That his presence is gift enough,
That someone chooses to notice
The man beneath the daily performance.

Your resolute tenderness becomes
The mirror where he finally glimpses
His own worthiness reflected back.
In loving him first, completely, consistently,
You give him permission to love himself.

This is the art of loving first—
Not waiting for reciprocation
But trusting that authentic appreciation,
Like water on stone,
Will eventually find its way through.

wrapping it all up: your journey starts now

Bringing It All Together: Creating a Climate of Desire **and Appreciation**

As we reach the conclusion of our exploration into the art of nonsexual foreplay (book 2!), it's worth reflecting on the larger truth these 75 gestures collectively reveal: meaningful intimacy isn't created through occasional grand gestures, but through consistent patterns of attention and care expressed in hundreds of small moments.

Think of these gestures not as isolated techniques to be mechanically implemented, but as expressions of an underlying mindset—one that prioritises ongoing connection over sporadic intensity, that values the ordinary moments as much as the extraordinary ones, and that recognises your partner's profound need for appreciation, acknowledgment, and affirmation.

Beyond Technique to Authentic Connection

The most powerful aspect of these gestures isn't their specific form but the genuine attention behind them. A mechanically perfect touch delivered without presence will always feel hollow compared to even the simplest gesture offered with complete authenticity. Your partner doesn't simply want your actions; he wants the quality of awareness that motivates them.

This is why developing genuine curiosity about his experience is so important. Rather than performing these gestures as obligation or strategy, approach them as opportunities to discover and appreciate the man before you—his unique responses, preferences, and emotional landscape. Let your natural desire to understand and connect with him guide which gestures you choose and how you adapt them to your particular relationship.

Creating Cycles of Positive Reinforcement

When consistently practiced, these gestures create a powerful virtuous cycle. As he feels genuinely appreciated and desired, he'll likely become more receptive, responsive, and demonstrative himself. This increased openness makes further connection easier and more natural, which in turn deepens the foundation of security and appreciation between you.

Remember that even when your expressions of appreciation or desire seem initially uncomfortable for him to receive, they're still registering and creating change. Many men have been conditioned to deflect recognition or downplay their need for affirmation. Your consistent, genuine acknowledgment helps create safety for him to gradually lower these defenses and embrace the appreciation he deeply craves.

Adapting to Your Unique Relationship

While this book offers 75 specific gestures, the most meaningful expressions will ultimately be the ones you discover together. Pay attention to which approaches resonate most powerfully for him, which forms of touch or acknowledgment create the strongest response, which words land most deeply. Then build on these discoveries, developing your own private language of connection uniquely suited to your relationship.

This process of discovery and adaptation keeps your connection fresh and responsive rather than formulaic. There's profound difference between following a script and dancing together, between reciting lines and having genuine conversation. Your willingness to observe, adapt, and create together ensures that your expressions of appreciation never become rote or predictable.

Consistency Matters More Than Perfection

Perhaps the most important principle to remember is that consistency matters far more than perfection. It's better to offer simple, authentic gestures regularly than elaborate expressions occasionally. The man in your life doesn't need flawless execution; he needs reliable evidence that he matters to you, that you see him, and that his presence in your life remains actively valued rather than merely accepted.

This consistency creates the foundation of security from which deeper intimacy naturally grows. When someone knows they are genuinely appreciated day after day, they develop the emotional safety necessary for vulnerability, playfulness, and authentic expression. Your regular acknowledgment helps create the conditions where both of you can be fully yourselves, without performance or pretense.

Physical Touch as Nourishment, Not Transaction

Many of the gestures in this book involve physical connection, and for good reason. Touch represents one of our most fundamental human needs—not just for pleasure but for wellbeing. Yet in many relationships, touch becomes either formalised into brief rituals or sexualised to the point where nonsexual physical connection diminishes significantly.

By reclaiming the territory of affectionate, sensual, appreciative touch that exists for its own sake rather than as prelude to something else, you're addressing a hunger that many men experience but rarely name. Your willingness to touch with presence and without expectation helps heal the touch deprivation that silently affects so many.

Here's a reminder. Hugs are good and should be part of every days morning and evening ritual!!

The Courage to Appreciate Openly

In a culture that often encourages emotional restraint, expressing genuine appreciation requires a certain courage. There's vulnerability in acknowledging how much someone means to you, in showing that you notice the details of who they are and how they move through the world.

Yet this courage creates extraordinary possibilities for connection. Your willingness to acknowledge what you value, to express what you desire, to show what you appreciate opens doors that remain closed in relationships characterised by emotional caution or restraint. Your openness creates permission for him to reciprocate, establishing patterns of mutual recognition that enrich your relationship in every dimension.

Beginning Your Practice

As you move forward from these pages into daily life with the man you care about, consider starting with the gestures that feel most natural and authentic to you. Perhaps choose one or two to practise consistently for a week, noticing how they affect both your experience and his response. Then gradually incorporate others, always with attention to what creates the most meaningful connection in your specific relationship.

Remember that even small shifts in how you express appreciation and desire can create significant changes over time. Just as compound interest transforms modest investments into substantial growth, your consistent gestures of acknowledgment and affection will gradually transform the emotional climate of your relationship.

The art of nonsexual foreplay isn't about performing for your partner's benefit, but about creating a relational space where both of you can thrive—where appreciation flows freely, where desire is expressed without agenda, where connection remains vibrant through all the seasons of life together. It's about discovering, again and again, the pleasure of truly seeing each other and being seen in return.

Your journey with these gestures is just beginning. May it lead you to ever deeper connection, mutual understanding and authentic intimacy with the man you've chosen to share your life and heart.

"Love has nothing to do with what you are expecting to get – only with what you are expecting to give – which is everything." – Katharine Hepburn

This quote captures the revolutionary shift at the heart of nonsexual foreplay—moving from transactional touch to transformational connection. When you stroke his face with genuine appreciation, play with his hair while watching television, or tell him specifically what you find attractive about him, you're embodying Hepburn's wisdom: expecting to give everything and receive nothing in return.

The magic happens when your gestures carry no hidden agenda, no silent expectation of reciprocation. When you reach for his hand in a crowded space or whisper something appreciative in his ear simply because you want to express your feelings, you're offering pure gift rather than down payment. This kind of generous love—love that gives everything and expects nothing—creates the very conditions where genuine intimacy can flourish. Paradoxically, when you stop expecting returns on your emotional investments, the returns often exceed anything you could have imagined.

Nolan Collins

what's next?

Don't forget! Here's how...

IF YOU'RE LIKE ME, YOU WANT TO DO BETTER, BUT OFTEN FORGET. I started putting reminders in my phone to do "something" but invariably forgot.

For that reason I now offer a Weekly "reminder" email for women that goes out with several suggestions of what you can do each week.

That's a lot of reminders of different things you can do. Some are mild, some are a bit more spicey.

Click here to sign up. It's only $19 per month or $97 per year. Less than Netflix and will do more for your relationship! https://nolancollins.com/aonsf2m

I also have books on:

Communication for couples: "The Connection Code"

Self Awareness: "BE" and "The Conversations My Parents Didn't Know To Have" (great for parents!)

And even Poetry - "Easy Poetry for Good Men" (coming late July 2025

visit https://nolancollins.com for details.

Courses

And if you want to be that calm, easy going, non reactive person you strive to be (when maybe he doesn't respond the way you want, and you feel like throwing the book at him!), take a look at my course on self mastery at https://nolancollins.com/5phases

about the author

Maybe I should have started with this so you know why I wrote this book.

My grandmother was a stickler for manners. She would stand next to a door waiting for me to open it. I was really young when she did this so I never took it the wrong way, and seeing the smile on her face and getting her polite "thank you" made me see that doing things for other people made them happy.

As a teenager dating, I often did those little things that made my girl friends smile, (and girlfriends!), and think this lanky boy with a funny accent was a nice guy.

As I got older, got married, and had kids, I realised that I forgot to do many of the things that are in the book, getting distracted with life, work, kids and the marriage.

After writing books about self-mastery, creating a book and tools on how to communicate better and a book on how to write poetry (for men!), I kept thinking about what my purpose is. I realised that it's threefold: to help people understand themselves, to help people communicate better, and to help couples stay together.

This is the first of several books on the last point.

I must admit I have a slight advantage in some areas as I learned to dance from a young age, even becoming a ballroom and swing dance instructor for a while, and I'm also a trained and qualified massage therapist! But you don't have to be either for this to work for you!

I love to see couples who are in love, especially elderly couples, and see them do things for each other selflessly.

Unfortunately I think more and more people come from homes where both parents work, and the only time parents show affection is in private, or when away from their kids. The art of connection has been lost over time and is at risk of disappearing like the dodo!

My teenage daughter frustratingly told me that the boys she was interested in had no manners, only thought about themselves or the one thing they were after. There was no finesse, no sensuality that didnt have the end goal of being intimate. For her, this was an immediate red flag.

So I've taken it on myself to teach the boys of the world, and now ladies, how to put their partner first, and learn all the ways they can do things for their partner to keep them happier, without the expectation of sex every time they do it.

My daugher knows what a gentleman looks like because she saw me do the things in this book.

Anyway, I believe everyone deserves to be happy, and it donesnt take much effort to do the small things that help every day feel a little lighter, feel appreciated, respected and adored.

If you're a man reading this, there's a companion book for men that can help you do things for your partner that will help her feel good about herself, the way you see her, and the relationship overall.

I wish you the best of luck in your life, love and relationships.

Nolan

www.ingramcontent.com/pod-product-compliance
Lightning Source LLC
Chambersburg PA
CBHW071221290326
41931CB00037B/1769